Copyright © 2021-All rights reserved.

No part of this publication may be reproduced, distributed, or transmitted in any form or by any means, including photocopying, recording, or other electronic or mechanical methods, without the prior written permission of the publisher, except in the case of brief quotations embodied in reviews and certain other non-commercial uses permitted by copyright law.

This Book is provided with the sole purpose of providing relevant information on a specific topic for which every reasonable effort has been made to ensure that it is both accurate and reasonable. Nevertheless, by purchasing this Book you consent to the fact that the author, as well as the publisher, are in no way experts on the topics contained herein, regardless of any claims as such that may be made within. It is recommended that you always consult a professional prior to undertaking any of the advice or techniques discussed with in.This is a legally binding declaration that is considered both valid and fair by both the Committee of Publishers Association and the American Bar Association and should be considered as legally binding within the United States.

CONTENTS

- **INTRODUCTION** 5
- **MORNING RECIPES** 7
  - Chicken Sandwiches with Barbecue Sauce 7
  - Savory Roast Beef Sandwiches 7
  - Buckwheat Pancake with Yogurt & Berries 8
  - Pumpkin Steel Cut Oats with Cinnamon 8
- **EGGS & VEGETABLES** 9
  - Curried Tofu with Vegetables 9
  - Asparagus & Mushrooms with Bacon 9
  - Green Vegetables with Tomatoes 10
  - Yummy Vegetable Soup 10
- **POULTRY** 11
  - Jamaican Chicken with Pineapple Sauce 11
  - Buffalo Chicken with Blue Cheese Sauce 11
  - Homemade Chicken Puttanesca 12
  - Sweet & Spicy BBQ Chicken 12
  - Fennel Chicken with Tomato Sauce 13
  - Chicken Gumbo 13
  - Sticky Teriyaki Chicken 14
  - Za'atar Chicken with Baby Potatoes 14
  - Indian-Style Chicken 15
  - Chicken with Chili & Lime 15
  - Cuban Mojo Chicken Tortillas 16
  - Creole Chicken with Rice 16
  - Moroccan-Style Chicken 17
  - Chicken in Creamy Mushroom Sauce ... 17
  - Peppered Chicken with Chunky Salsa . 18
  - Chicken & Bacon Cacciatore 18
  - Lemon & Thyme Chicken 19
  - Cumin Chicken with Capers 19
  - Feta Cheese Turkey Balls 20
  - Chicken with Port Wine Sauce 20
  - Turkey Cakes with Ginger Gravy 21
  - Delicious Turkey Burgers 22
  - Rigatoni with Turkey & Tomato Sauce 22
  - Sunday Turkey Lettuce Wraps 23
  - Homemade Turkey Pepperoni Pizza ... 23
  - Turkish-Style Roasted Turkey 24
  - Spicy Turkey Casserole with Tomatoes 24
  - Cranberry Turkey with Hazelnuts 25
  - Parsley & Lemon Turkey Risotto 25
  - Sage Turkey & Red Wine Casserole 26
  - Spicy Ground Turkey Chili with Vegetables 26
  - Turkey & Black Bean Chili 27
  - Turkey Stew with Salsa Verde 27
  - Potato Skins with Shredded Turkey 28
  - Turkey Soup with Noodle 28
  - Caribbean Turkey Wings 29
  - Turkey Meatball Soup with Rice 30
  - Hungarian-Style Turkey Stew 31
  - Buffalo Turkey Chili 31
  - Turkey Sausage with Brussels Sprouts 32
  - Potato & Cauliflower Turkey Soup 32
  - North African Turkey Stew 33
  - Weekend Turkey with Vegetables 33
  - Turkey with Rice & Peas 34
  - Mediterranean Duck with Olives 34
  - Honey-Glazed Turkey 35
  - Roast Goose with White Wine 35
  - Duck Breasts with Honey-Mustard Glaze 36
- **PORK** 37
  - Awesome Pork & Celery Soup 37
  - Delicious Pork & Vegetables Soup 37
  - Cajun Orange Pork Shoulder 38
  - Garlic & Thyme Pork 39
  - German-Style Red Cabbage with Apples 40
  - Gruyere Mushroom & Mortadella Cups 40
  - Asparagus Wrapped in Parma Ham 41
  - Ranch Potatoes with Ham 41

BEEF & LAMB ... 42
- Easy Lamb & Spinach Soup ... 42
- Roast Lamb Leg with Potatoes ... 42
- Lamb Shanks with Garlic & Thyme ... 43
- Lamb with Tomato & Green Peas ... 43
- Minty Lamb ... 44
- Hot Paprika & Oregano Lamb ... 45
- Mediterranean Lamb ... 46
- Quick French-Style Lamb with Sesame 46
- Lamb Stew with Lemon & Parsley ... 47
- Simple Roast Lamb ... 47
- Traditional Lamb with Vegetables ... 48
- Garlic Lamb with Thyme ... 48
- Leg of Lamb with Garlic and Pancetta . 49
- Savory Irish Lamb Stew ... 49
- Asian-Style Lamb Curry ... 50
- Spicy Lamb & Bean Chili ... 51
- Fennel Lamb Ribs ... 51
- Lamb Chops with Mashed Potatoes ... 52
- Vegetable & Lamb Casserole ... 53
- Balsamic Lamb ... 54
- Lamb Chorba ... 54

FISH & SEAFOOD ... 55
- Chinese Shrimp with Green Beans ... 55
- Cheesy Shrimp Scampi ... 55
- Indian Prawn Curry ... 56
- Butter & Wine Lobster Tails ... 56
- Ginger & Garlic Crab ... 57
- Herby Crab Legs with Lemon ... 57
- Black Squid Ink Tagliatelle ... 58
- Crab Pilaf with Broccoli & Asparagus .. 58
- Red Wine Squid ... 59
- White Wine Marinated Squid Rings ... 59
- Mussels With Lemon & White Wine ... 60
- Chili Squid ... 60
- Spicy Mussels & Anchovies with Rice .. 61
- Beer-Steamed Mussels ... 61
- Basil Clams with Garlic & White Wine. 62
- Saucy Clams with Herbs ... 62
- Clam & Corn Chowder ... 63
- Lime & Honey Scallops ... 63
- Octopus & Shrimp with Collard Greens ... 64
- Galician-Style Octopus ... 64
- White Wine Oysters ... 65

PASTA & RICE ... 66
- Coconut Rice Breakfast ... 66
- Prawn Basmati Rice ... 66
- Pomegranate Rice with Vegetables ... 67
- Hazelnut Brown Rice Pilaf ... 67
- Vegetable Green Biryani ... 68
- Wild Rice Pilaf ... 68
- Spicy Indian Rice ... 69
- Pilau Brown Rice ... 69
- Rice & Red Bean Pot ... 70
- Rice & Chicken Soup ... 70
- One-Pot Mexican Rice ... 71

BEANS & GRAINS ... 72
- Apricot Steel Cut Oats ... 72
- Honey Oat & Pumpkin Granola ... 72
- Kiwi Steel Cut Oatmeal ... 73
- Southern Cheese Grits ... 73
- Coconut Cherry Steel Cut Oats ... 73
- Jamaican Cornmeal Porridge ... 74
- Cheesy Polenta with Sundried Tomatoes ... 74
- Garlic Mushroom Polenta ... 75

APPETIZERS & SIDE DISHES ... 76
- Potatoes & Tuna Salad with Pickles ... 76
- Grandma's Egg Salad ... 76
- Arugula Salad with Sweet Potatoes & Eggs ... 77
- Authentic German Salad with Bacon ... 77
- Delicious Broccoli & Cauliflower Salad ... 78
- Greek-Style Pasta Salad ... 78

BROTHS & SAUCES ... 79
- Herbed Squash Sauce ... 79
- Garlic Red Bell Pepper Sauce ... 79
- Quick Zucchini Sauce with Greek Yogurt ... 80
- Mediterranean Tomato Sauce ... 80
- Caprese Sauce with Goat Cheese ... 81
- Homemade Honey Applesauce ... 81

- Spicy Green Sauce 81

SOUPS 82
- Corn Soup with Chicken & Egg 82
- Mustard Carrot Soup..............................82
- Easy Veggie Soup 83
- Cheesy & Creamy Broccoli Soup 83
- Gingery Carrot Soup...............................84
- Carrot & Cabbage Soup 84
- Scallion Chicken & Lentil Soup 85
- Tomato Shrimp Soup 85
- Mustard Potato Soup with Crispy Bacon 86
- Curried Pumpkin Soup...........................86
- Nutmeg Broccoli Soup with Cheddar ...87
- Kielbasa Sausage Soup 87
- Chorizo & Bean Soup.............................88
- Beet & Potato Soup...............................88
- Vegan Tomato Soup...............................89
- Asian Tomato Soup................................89
- Tangy Pumpkin Soup.............................90
- Chicken Soup with Vegetables...............90
- Celery & Oxtail Soup..............................91
- Creamy Mushroom Soup with Chicken 91
- Cheesy Cauliflower Soup 92
- Spicy Ground Beef Soup.........................92
- Hot Spinach Soup...................................93
- Asian-Style Chicken Soup.......................93
- Egg & Chicken Soup................................94
- Cheesy Chicken Soup..............................94
- Brussel Sprout & Pork Soup....................95
- Tamarind Beef Soup................................95
- Cashew & Tomato Soup..........................96
- Pecorino Mushroom Soup 96
- Creamy Chicken & Zucchini Soup...........97
- Quick Chicken Soup 97
- Chicken & Noodle Soup..........................98
- Simple Onion Cheese Soup 98

STEWS 99
- Rabbit & Veggie Stew................................. 99
- Thyme Chicken Pot with Cheese.........100
- Coconut & Cauliflower Curry...............100
- Pancetta & Cheese Chicken Thighs 101
- Habanero Chicken Stew.......................101
- Chinese-Style Chicken Stew with Broccoli...102
- Hot Beef Chili......................................102
- Delicious Thai Vegetable Stew............103
- Garbanzo Stew with Onions & Tomatoes..103

VEGAN & VEGETARIAN.............................104
- Vegan Sloppy Joe's 104
- Sweet Polenta with Pistachios 104
- Almond & Cherry Millet.......................105
- Basil Parmesan Sauce 105
- Coconut Milk Millet Pudding 105
- Blueberry & Quinoa Porridge..............106
- Carrot & Sweet Potato Thick Soup.....106
- Coconut Millet Porridge......................106
- Cheddar Cheese Sauce with Broccoli 107
- Hot Tofu Meatballs...............................107

DESSERTS & DRINKS...............................108
- Amazing Fruity Cheesecake 108
- Chocolate Quinoa Bowl 108
- Simple Apple Cider with Orange Juice 109
- Spiced & Warming Mulled Wine 109
- Walnut & Dark Chocolate Brownies..110
- Quick Coconut Treat with Pears.........110
- Homemade Walnut Layer Cake 111
- Creme Caramel with Whipped Cream..111
- Plum & Almond Dessert.......................111

APPENDIX : RECIPES INDEX.....................112

INTRODUCTION

Instant Pot is a magic pot which can transform a few, affordable ingredients into the most delicious dinner in the fastest and easiest way. If you are about to start using the Instant Pot that will be one of the best companion in your journey to a healthier and happier life. Even if you have a tight schedule, you can always find 5-10 minutes to prepare a bunch of ingredients and put them in the pot. You can steam the baby carrots, cook the lentils or produce the homemade yogurt from one single touch of the display. Instant Pot will make you love the world of food, so you will be more successful in sticking to your diet with way less efforts.

During the last century, the food industry provided us with too many options of tasty, but unhealthy processed foods full of artificial additives, colors, and preservatives. Long-term consumption of such products resulted in worsening health conditions of the population, so it's time to make a change. Home cooking can prevent the development of diabetes, stroke and heart failure, and it can also normalize blood pressure and cholesterol levels. Moreover, this magnificent cooking appliance can be used as a safe and effective tool for improving weight loss.

If you are reading this page, it means that you have already decided to start better eating habits and you chose the one of the healthies and fastest way to prepare the food - the Instant Pot pressure cooker. I congratulate you with the right choice to change your life for the better. This book contains 1000 recipes which will help you enjoy mouthwatering and healthy meals, everyday and for any occasion for the whole family and friends.

Why The Instant Pot is Great to Have

Sometimes it's easier to buy ready-to-eat sausages in the supermarket or a quick cheesy burger at burger king. The combination of various unnatural additives, huge amounts of monosodium glutamate and sugar ruin the digestive system and affect some organs. Nothing bad will happen because of one or two "cheat meals", but repetetive consumption of processed foods over the course of months and years will affect you and your health.

The second thing you should do is to change your shopping behavior and buy fresh, organic and quality products so you can start cooking at home. I promise that you will find tons of mouthwatering recipes in this book which will excite you to cook and forget about the quick sugary snacks.

One-Touch Cooking Modes of Instant Pot

Instant Pot Pressure Cooker is your best friend in the kitchen that will help you immensely to achieve freedom in your kitchen - quickly and effortlessly. Thanks to one-touch cooking modes, the Instant Pot saves a lot of time and energy, and rewards you with tasty and nutritious meals.

- **Soup/Broth**. This pre-set method is for cooking soups or broths.
- **Meat/Stew**. This mode will be useful for stewing almost all kind of vegetables including peas, zucchini, spinach and other leafy veggies along with some juicy beef or park stew meat
- **Beans/Chili**. Lentils and beans are healthy plant-based sources of protein, so this setting will help you cook them in the fastest and hassle-free way.

- **Poultry.** Chicken and turkey should be prepared under this cooking mode. The meat will cook itself becoming tender and juicy.
- **Rice.** While rice is not considered as a part of the 20 healthiest foods, yet you can still utilize this setting for cooking quinoa or other nutritious grains.
- **Multigrain.** Wholegrains are full of the fiber, micro and macro elements, so you must add them to your everyday meals. The Instant Pot significantly reduces the cooking time of whole grains in comparison to a standard oven.
- **Porridge.** Tasty and nutritive oatmeal is a great way to start your day. This mode will help you cook the perfect breakfast.
- **Steam**. Steaming is the safest and the most effective cooking method, since it maximizes the amount of antioxidants and fiber in the food.
- **Sauté.** This mode allows stir-frying, browning or searing veggies, meat, poultry of fish.
- **Yogurt**. The best option for a homemade low-fat yogurt. When cooked at home, the yogurt is a very healthy food, without any added sugars and preservatives.
- **Pressure cook/Manual mode -** this is the most important Instant Pot setting. You can use this function for any kind of food preparation and adjust the pressure and cooking time as needed.
- **Slow cook**. The Instant Pot can also function as a Slow cooker. If you have plenty of time before a dinner, this method will help you to prepare the most delicious and tasty stews.
- **Pressure Level**. Depending on the amount of ingredients and their properties, you can adjust higher or lower pressure level to ensure the best cooking results.
- **Delay start.** You have a busy day and don't want to spend morning time in the kitchen? No problem, just prepare the ingredients, throw them in the Pot and set it to start cooking in 8h. And the dinner will be ready just in time. This function is also handy for soaking beans/grains.
- **Keep warm.** This function keeps the food warm. No need to microwave the meal anymore.

Note! Some Instant Pot models may have slightly different functions or buttons. Always check the manufacturer's manual before using any setting on your pressure cooker.

MORNING RECIPES

Chicken Sandwiches with Barbecue Sauce

Serving Size: 4 | **Total Time:** 50 minutes

4 chicken thighs, boneless and skinless
2 cups barbecue sauce
1 onion, minced
2 garlic cloves, minced
2 tbsp minced fresh parsley
1 tbsp lemon juice
1 tbsp mayonnaise
2 cups lettuce, shredded
4 burger buns

Into the pot, place the garlic, onion, and barbecue sauce. Add in the chicken and toss it to coat. Seal the lid and cook on High Pressure for 15 minutes. Do a natural release for 10 minutes. Use two forks to shred the chicken and mix it into the sauce. Press Keep Warm and let the mixture simmer for 15 minutes to thicken the sauce until the desired consistency.

In a bowl, mix lemon juice, mayonnaise, and parsley; toss lettuce into the mixture to coat. Separate the chicken into equal parts to match the burger buns; top with lettuce and complete the sandwiches.

Savory Roast Beef Sandwiches

Serving Size: 8 | **Total Time:** 1 hour 30 minutes

2 ½ lb beef roast
2 tbsp olive oil
1 onion, chopped
4 garlic cloves, minced
½ cup dry red wine
2 cups beef broth stock
16 slices Fontina cheese
8 split hoagie rolls
Salt and pepper to taste

Season the beef with salt and pepper. Warm oil on Sauté and brown the beef for 2 to 3 minutes per side; reserve. Add onion and garlic to the pot and cook for 3 minutes until translucent. Set aside. Add red wine to deglaze. Mix in beef broth and take back the beef. Seal the lid and cook on High Pressure for 50 minutes. Release the pressure naturally for 10 minutes. Preheat a broiler. Transfer the beef to a cutting board and slice. Roll the meat and top with onion. Each sandwich should be topped with 2 Fontina cheese slices. Place the sandwiches under the broiler for 2-3 minutes until the cheese melts.

Buckwheat Pancake with Yogurt & Berries

Serving Size: 4 | **Total Time:** 15 minutes

1 cup buckwheat flour
2 tsp baking powder
1 ¼ cups milk
1 egg
1 tsp vanilla sugar
1 tsp strawberry extract
1 cup Greek yogurt
1 cup fresh berries

In a bowl, whisk milk and egg until foamy. Gradually add flour and continue to beat until combined. Add baking powder, strawberry extract, and vanilla sugar. Spoon the batter in a greased cake pan. Pour 1 cup of water into the pot. Place a trivet. Lay the pan on the trivet. Seal the lid and cook for 5 minutes on High Pressure. Do a quick release. Top pancake with yogurt and berries.

Pumpkin Steel Cut Oats with Cinnamon

Serving Size: 4 | **Total Time:** 25 minutes

1 tbsp butter
2 cups steel-cut oats
¼ tsp cinnamon
1 cup pumpkin puree
3 tbsp maple syrup
2 tsp pumpkin seeds, toasted

Melt butter on Sauté. Add in cinnamon, oats, pumpkin puree, and 3 cups of water. Seal the lid, select Porridge and cook for 10 minutes on High Pressure to get a few bite oats or for 14 minutes to form soft oats. Do a quick release. Open the lid and stir in maple syrup. Top with pumpkin seeds and serve.

EGGS & VEGETABLES

Curried Tofu with Vegetables

Serving Size: 4 | **Total Time:** 20 minutes

2 tbsp sesame oil
3 green onions, sliced
3 garlic cloves, minced
1 celery stalk, chopped
1 cup mushrooms, sliced
1 red bell pepper, chopped
¼ tsp curry powder
28 oz firm tofu, cubed
1 cup bbq sauce
1 tbsp sesame seeds, toasted

Warm the sesame oil in your Instant Pot on Sauté. Place the green onions, garlic celery, mushrooms, and bell pepper and cook for 3 minutes. Stir in salt and curry powder and cook for 2 more minutes.

Add in tofu, and bbq sauce, and ½ cup of water. Seal the lid, select Manual, and cook for 5 minutes on High. Once ready, perform a quick pressure release and unlock the lid. Serve warm topped with sesame seeds.

Asparagus & Mushrooms with Bacon

Serving Size: 4 | **Total Time:** 30 minutes

1 lb asparagus, trimmed
6 oz bacon, chopped
1 clove garlic, minced
1 yellow onion, chopped
8 oz mushrooms, sliced
Salt and pepper to taste
1 tbsp balsamic vinegar

Place asparagus in your Instant Pot and pour in water. Seal the lid, select Manual, and cook for 3 minutes on High pressure. When ready, allow a natural release for 10 minutes and unlock the lid. Strain asparagus; set aside.

Press Sauté on the pot and add bacon; cook for 1-2 minutes. Stir in garlic and onion and sauté for 2 minutes. Mix in mushrooms and cook until they are soft. Mix in cooked asparagus, salt, pepper, and balsamic vinegar and combine. Serve immediately.

Green Vegetables with Tomatoes

Serving Size: 6 | **Total Time**: 15 minutes

1 tsp olive oil
1 clove garlic, minced
2 cups chopped tomatoes
½ cup vegetable stock
½ lb green beans, trimmed
½ cup green peas
½ lb asparagus, trimmed
Salt and pepper to taste

Warm the olive oil in your Instant Pot on Sauté. Place in garlic and cook for 30 seconds until fragrant. Stir in tomatoes. Pour in vegetable stock, green beans, green peas, and asparagus; season with salt, and pepper. Seal the lid, select Manual, and cook for 5 minutes on High pressure. When done, perform a quick pressure release.

Yummy Vegetable Soup

Serving Size: 4 | **Total Time**: 25 minutes

2 tbsp olive oil
1 cup leeks, chopped
2 garlic cloves, minced
4 cups vegetable stock
1 carrot, diced
1 parsnip, diced
1 celery stalk, diced
1 cup mushrooms
1 cup broccoli florets
1 cup cauliflower florets
½ red bell pepper, diced
¼ head cabbage, chopped
½ cup green beans
2 tbsp nutritional yeast
Salt and pepper to taste
½ cup parsley, chopped

Heat oil on Sauté. Add in garlic and leeks and cook for 6 minutes until slightly browned. Add in stock, carrot, celery, broccoli, bell pepper, green beans, salt, nutritional yeast, cabbage, cauliflower, mushrooms, parsnip, and pepper. Seal the lid and cook on High Pressure for 6 minutes. Release pressure naturally. Stir in parsley to serve.

POULTRY

Jamaican Chicken with Pineapple Sauce

Serving Size: 4 | **Total Time:** 40 minutes

1 lb chicken thighs
½ cup coconut cream
2 tbsp soy sauce
1 cup pineapple chunks
1 tsp Jamaican seasoning
1 tsp coriander seeds
¼ tsp salt
½ cup cilantro, chopped
1 tsp arrowroot starch

Place chicken thighs, coconut cream, soy sauce, Jamaican jerk seasoning, coriander seeds, and salt in your Instant Pot and stir. Pour in 1 cup of water and seal the lid; cook for 15 minutes on manual. Once over, allow a natural release for 10 minutes and unlock the lid.

Remove chicken to a bowl. Combine arrowroot starch and 1 tbsp of water in a cup and pour it into the pot. Add in pineapple chunks and cook for 4-5 minutes on Sauté. Top the chicken with cilantro and sauce. Serve.

Buffalo Chicken with Blue Cheese Sauce

Serving Size: 4 | **Total Time:** 30 minutes

1 lb chicken breasts, cut into thin strips
2 tbsp olive oil
1 tsp paprika
1 yellow onion, chopped
½ cup celery, chopped
½ cup buffalo sauce
½ cup chicken stock
¼ cup blue cheese, crumbled
4 tbsp sour cream

Place the chicken breasts, olive oil, paprika, onion, celery, buffalo sauce, and chicken stock in your Instant Pot. Seal the lid, select Manual, and cook for 12 minutes on High.

When ready, allow a natural release for 10 minutes and unlock the lid. In a bowl, combine the crumbled blue cheese and sour cream and add 1 cup of the cooking juice and stir. Pour into the pot. Serve right away.

Homemade Chicken Puttanesca

Serving Size: 6 | **Total Time:** 45 minutes

6 chicken thighs, skin on
2 tbsp olive oil
2 anchovy fillets, chopped
14 oz canned diced tomatoes
2 garlic cloves, crushed
½ tsp red chili flakes
6 oz pitted black olives
1 tbsp capers
1 tbsp fresh basil, chopped
Salt and pepper to taste

Warm the olive oil in your Instant Pot on Sauté. Place in the chicken thighs skin side-down and brown for 4-6 minutes. Remove to a bowl. Place tomatoes, garlic, chili flakes, anchovy fillets, black olives, capers, fresh basil, salt, and pepper into the pot. Pour in 1 cup of water.

Bring to a simmer. Add in back the chicken and seal the lid. Select Manual and cook for 20 minutes on High pressure. When ready, allow a natural release for 10 minutes and unlock the lid. Serve immediately.

Sweet & Spicy BBQ Chicken

Serving Size: 4 | **Total Time:** 35 minutes

6 chicken drumsticks
1 tbsp olive oil
1 onion, chopped
1 tsp garlic, minced
1 jalapeño pepper, minced
½ cup sweet BBQ sauce
1 tbsp arrowroot

Warm the olive oil in your Instant Pot on Sauté. Add in the onion and cook for 3 minutes. Add in garlic and jalapeño pepper and cook for another minute. Stir in barbecue sauce and 1/2 cup of water. Put in chicken drumsticks and seal the lid. Select Manual and cook for 18 minutes on High pressure. When over, perform a quick pressure release and unlock the lid. Mix 2 tbsp of water and arrowroot and pour it into the pot. Cook for 5 minutes on Sauté until the liquid thickens. Top with sauce and serve.

Fennel Chicken with Tomato Sauce

Serving Size: 4 | **Total Time:** 35 minutes

1 lb chicken breasts
½ cup chicken broth
Salt and pepper to taste
1 tbsp fennel seeds
2 tbsp olive oil
2 cups tomato-basil sauce

Place the chicken breasts, olive oil, chicken broth, fennel seeds, salt, and pepper in your Instant Pot. Seal the lid, select Manual, and cook for 20 minutes on High pressure. When done, perform a quick pressure release and unlock the lid. Shred the chicken and add in tomato sauce. Simmer for 5 minutes on Saute. Serve immediately.

Chicken Gumbo

Serving Size: 4 | **Total Time:** 40 minutes

4 chicken thighs
1 onion, diced
2 garlic cloves, minced
2 sticks celery, finely diced
2 green peppers, diced
1 tsp Cajun seasoning
Salt and pepper to taste
2 tbsp olive oil
1 ½ cups tomato sauce
1 jalapeno, halved
2 tbsp sage, chopped

Warm the olive oil in your Instant Pot on Sauté. Place in chicken and cook for 4-6 minutes on all sides; reserve. Add in onion, garlic, celery, and green peppers and cook for 5 minutes. Stir in Cajun seasoning, tomato sauce, salt, pepper, and 1 cup of water. Seal the lid, select Manual, and cook for 20 minutes on High pressure. When ready, perform a quick pressure release and unlock the lid. Top with sage and jalapeño pepper and serve.

Sticky Teriyaki Chicken

Serving Size: 4 | **Total Time:** 30 minutes

1 lb chicken breasts
2/3 cup teriyaki sauce
1 tsp sesame seeds
½ cup chicken stock
Salt and pepper to taste
3 green onions, chopped

Set your Instant Pot to Sauté. Place in teriyaki sauce and simmer for 1 minute. Stir in chicken stock, salt, and pepper and seal the lid. Select Manual and cook for 12 minutes on High pressure. Once over, allow a natural release for 10 minutes and unlock the lid. Transfer the chicken to a plate and shred it. Remove 1/2 cup of cooking liquid. Put chicken back in the pot and stir in green onions. Top with sesame seeds and serve.

Za'atar Chicken with Baby Potatoes

Serving Size: 4 | **Total Time:** 30 minutes

1 lb chicken thighs
½ lb baby potatoes, halved
2 tbsp olive oil
1 tbsp za'atar seasoning
1 garlic clove, minced
1 large onion, sliced
Salt and pepper to taste

Warm the olive oil in your Instant Pot on Sauté. Place in onion and garlic and cook for 2 minutes. Add in chicken thighs and cook for 4-6 minutes on both sides. Scatter with za´atar seasoning, salt, pepper, potatoes, and pour in 1 cup of water. Seal the lid, select Manual, and cook for 15 minutes on High pressure.

Once ready, perform a quick pressure release and unlock the lid. Remove the chicken and shred it. Put chicken back to the pot and toss to coat. Serve right away.

Indian-Style Chicken

Serving Size: 6 | **Total Time**: 37 minutes + marinating time

6 chicken thighs, bone-in
½ cup Greek yogurt
1 tbsp curry paste
1 tbsp lemon juice
Salt and pepper to taste
1 tbsp fresh ginger, grated
2 tbsp cilantro, chopped

Combine yogurt, lemon juice, curry paste, salt, and pepper in a bowl. Add in chicken thighs and toss to coat. Let marinate in the fridge for 2 hours. Place the chicken, marinade, ginger, and 1 cup of water in your Instant Pot. Seal the lid, select Manual, and cook for 12 minutes on High pressure. When over, allow a natural release for 10 minutes and unlock the lid. Transfer to a baking tray and put under the broiler 3-5 minutes. Top with cilantro.

Chicken with Chili & Lime

Serving Size: 4 | **Total Time**: 25 minutes

1 lb chicken breasts
¾ cup chicken broth
Juice and zest of 1 lime
1 red chili, chopped
1 tsp cumin
1 tsp onion powder
2 garlic cloves, minced
1 tsp mustard powder
1 bay leaf
Salt and pepper to taste

Place the chicken breasts, chicken broth, lime juice, lime zest, red chili, cumin, onion powder, garlic cloves, mustard powder, bay leaf, salt, and pepper in your Instant Pot. Seal the lid, select Manual, and cook for 10 minutes on High. When ready, allow a natural release. Remove chicken and shred it. Discard the bay leaf. Top the chicken with cooking juices and serve.

Cuban Mojo Chicken Tortillas

Serving Size: 4 | **Total Time:** 80 minutes + marinating time

4 chicken breasts
2 tbsp olive oil
1 lime, juiced
1 grapefruit, juiced
4 garlic cloves, minced
1 tsp ground cumin
Salt and pepper to taste
2 tbsp chopped cilantro
4 tortillas
1 avocado, sliced
2 tbsp hot sauce

Combine olive oil, lime juice, grapefruit juice, garlic, cumin, cilantro, salt, and pepper in a bowl. Add in chicken breasts and let marinate covered for 30 minutes. Transfer chicken and marinade to your Instant Pot and pour in 1 cup of water. Seal the lid and cook for 20 minutes on Manual. Once done, allow a natural release for 10 minutes and unlock the lid. Remove the chicken and shred it, then add it back to the pot; stir. Divide the chicken between the tortillas and top with avocado slices and hot sauce. Serve right away.

Creole Chicken with Rice

Serving Size: 4 | **Total Time:** 45 minutes

2 tbsp olive oil
1 onion, diced
3 garlic cloves, minced
1 lb chicken breasts, sliced
1 cup chicken broth
1 (14.5-oz) can tomato sauce
1 cup white rice, rinsed
1 bell pepper, chopped
2 tsp creole seasoning
1 tbsp hot sauce

Warm the olive oil in your Instant Pot on Sauté. Place in onion and garlic and cook until fragrant, about 3 minutes. Stir in chicken breasts, bell pepper, hot sauce, and creole seasoning. Cook for 3 more minutes. Mix in chicken broth, tomato sauce, and rice and seal the lid. Select Manual and cook for 20 minutes on High pressure. When ready, allow a natural release for 10 minutes and unlock the lid. Serve warm.

Moroccan-Style Chicken

Serving Size: 4 | **Total Time:** 30 minutes

1 lb chicken thighs, skinless
2 tbsp vegetable oil
Salt and pepper to taste
3 garlic cloves, minced
1 large onion, chopped
¼ tsp cumin
½ cup chicken broth
12 dried apricots, sliced
1 lb canned tomatoes, diced
1 tbsp fresh ginger, grated
½ tsp cinnamon, ground
2 tbsp cilantro, chopped
2 tbsp flaked almonds

Warm the vegetable oil in your Instant Pot on Sauté. Sprinkle chicken thighs with salt and pepper and place in the pot along with garlic and onion. Cook for 5 minutes. Stir in chicken broth, apricots, tomatoes, fresh ginger, cumin, and cinnamon. Seal the lid, select Manual, and cook for 12 minutes on High pressure. Once ready, perform a quick pressure release and unlock the lid. Serve topped with cilantro and almonds.

Chicken in Creamy Mushroom Sauce

Serving Size: 4 | **Total Time:** 50 minutes

1 lb chicken breasts
1 tbsp olive oil
1 cup mushrooms, sliced
1 large onion, chopped
2 garlic cloves, minced
1 cup chicken stock
Salt and pepper to taste
1 cup heavy cream
2 green onions, chopped

Warm the olive oil in your Instant Pot on Sauté. Place in mushrooms, onion, and garlic and cook for 4-5 minutes. Sprinkle chicken breasts with salt and pepper and place in the pot. Cook for 6-8 minutes on all sides. Add in chicken stock and stir. Seal the lid, select Manual, and cook for 12 minutes on High pressure.

Once done, allow a natural release for 10 minutes. Remove the chicken. Add the heavy cream to the cooker and stir for 3 minutes on Sauté. Pour the sauce over the chicken, top with green onions, and serve warm.

Peppered Chicken with Chunky Salsa

Serving Size: 4 | **Total Time:** 30 minutes

3 mixed-color peppers, cut into strips
1 lb chicken breasts
2 tbsp olive oil
2 jalapeño peppers, sliced
1 onion, sliced
Salt and pepper to taste
½ tsp oregano
½ tsp cumin
2 cups chunky salsa

Warm the olive oil in your Instant Pot on Sauté. Place in onion, peppers, and jalapeño peppers and sauté for 5 minutes. Sprinkle chicken breasts with salt and pepper and place them in the pot along with oregano, cumin, chunky salsa, and ½ cup of water. Seal the lid and cook for 15 minutes on Manual on High. When ready, perform a quick pressure release. Shred chicken before serving.

Chicken & Bacon Cacciatore

Serving Size: 4 | **Total Time:** 45 minutes

2 cups canned tomatoes and juice, crushed
1 lb chicken drumsticks
4 oz bacon, chopped
1 red onion, chopped
1 cup chicken stock
1 garlic clove, minced
1 tsp oregano, dried
1 bay leaf
Salt to taste
1 roasted pepper, chopped
12 Kalamata olives, sliced

Set your Instant Pot to Sauté. Add in the bacon and cook for 5 minutes. Stir in onion and garlic and cook for 3 minutes. Pour in chicken stock, tomatoes, oregano, bay leaf, salt, and chicken. Seal the lid, select Manual, and cook for 15 minutes on High pressure. Once over, allow a natural release for 10 minutes and unlock the lid. Discard the bay leaf and mix in roasted pepper. Serve topped with olives.

Lemon & Thyme Chicken

Serving Size: 6 | **Total Time**: 40 minutes

3 lb red potatoes, peeled and quartered
2 lb chicken thighs
2 tbsp olive oil
1 onion, chopped
2 garlic cloves, minced
2 tbsp thyme, chopped
¾ cup chicken broth
1 lemon, juiced and zested
Salt and pepper to taste

Warm the olive oil in your Instant Pot on Sauté. Place in the chicken thighs and brown for 2-3 minutes, stirring occasionally. Add in onion and garlic and cook for 3 minutes. Stir in chicken broth, lemon zest, lemon juice, potatoes, half of the thyme, salt, and pepper. Seal the lid and cook for 15 minutes on Poultry. Once ready, allow a natural release for 10 minutes and unlock the lid. Top with thyme and serve.

Cumin Chicken with Capers

Serving Size: 4 | **Total Time**: 30 minutes

4 chicken breasts
½ cup butter
½ tsp cumin
Salt and pepper to taste
Juice of 1 lemon
1 cup chicken broth
½ cup capers

Melt butter in your Instant Pot on Sauté. Sprinkle chicken breasts with cumin, salt, and pepper and place in the pot. Cook for 7-8 minutes on all sides. Stir in lemon juice, chicken broth, and capers and seal the lid. Select Manual and cook for 10 minutes on High pressure. Once ready, allow a natural release for 5 minutes and unlock the lid.

Feta Cheese Turkey Balls

Serving Size: 6 | **Total Time:** 35 minutes

1 onion, minced
½ cup plain bread crumbs
1/3 cup feta, crumbled
Salt and pepper to taste
½ tsp dried oregano
1 lb ground turkey
1 egg, lightly beaten
1 tbsp olive oil
1 carrot, minced
½ celery stalk, minced
3 cups tomato puree
2 cups water

In a mixing bowl, combine half the onion, oregano, turkey, salt, crumbs, pepper, and egg, and stir until everything is well incorporated. Heat oil on Sauté in your Instant Pot. Cook celery, remaining onion, and carrot for 5 minutes until soft. Pour in water and tomato puree. Adjust the seasonings. Roll the mixture into meatballs, and drop into the sauce. Seal the lid. Press Meat/Stew and cook on High Pressure for 5 minutes. Release the pressure naturally for 20 minutes. Serve topped with feta.

Chicken with Port Wine Sauce

Serving Size: 6 | **Total Time:** 41 minutes

1 (3 lb) chicken, cut into pieces
2 tbsp olive oil
1 large onion, finely diced
1 cup mushrooms
¼ cup Port wine
Salt and pepper to taste
2 tbsp parsley, chopped

Warm olive oil in your IP on Sauté. Add in the chicken pieces and cook until the chicken is light brown, about 6-7 minutes; set aside. Add onion and mushrooms to the pot and sauté for 3-4 minutes. Deglaze with Port wine and pour in 1 cup of water. Season with salt and pepper and return the chicken. Seal the lid, select Manual, and cook for 20 minutes on High. Once ready, release pressure naturally. Sprinkle with parsley and serve.

Turkey Cakes with Ginger Gravy

Serving Size: 4 | **Total Time**: 25 minutes

1 lb ground turkey
¼ cup breadcrumbs
¼ cup grated Parmesan
½ tsp garlic powder
2 green onions, chopped
Salt and pepper to taste
2 tbsp olive oil
2 cups tomatoes, diced
¼ cup chicken broth

GINGER SAUCE

4 tbsp soy sauce
2 tbsp canola oil
2 tbsp rice vinegar
1 garlic clove, minced
1 tsp ginger, grated
½ tbsp honey
¼ tsp black pepper
½ tbsp cornstarch

Combine turkey, breadcrumbs, green onions, garlic powder, salt, pepper, and Parmesan cheese in a bowl. Mix with your hands and shape meatballs out of the mixture. In another bowl, mix soy sauce, canola oil, rice vinegar, garlic clove, ginger, honey, pepper, and cornstarch. Warm the olive oil in your Instant Pot on Sauté.

Place in meatballs and cook for 4 minutes on all sides. Pour in ginger gravy, tomatoes, and chicken stock and seal the lid. Select Manual and cook for 10 minutes on High pressure. Once over, perform a quick pressure release and unlock the lid. Serve in individual bowls.

Delicious Turkey Burgers

Serving Size: 4 | **Total Time:** 35 minutes

1 lb ground turkey
2 egg
1 tbsp flour
1 onion, finely chopped
Salt and pepper to taste
1 tbsp sour cream

In a bowl, add ground turkey, egg, flour, onion, salt, pepper, and sour cream and mix well. Form the mixture into patties. Line parchment paper over a baking dish and arrange the patties. Pour 1 cup of water into your Instant Pot. Lay the trivet and place the baking dish on top.

Seal the lid. Cook on Manual for 15 minutes on High. Release the pressure naturally for 10 minutes. Unlock the lid. Serve with lettuce and tomatoes.

Rigatoni with Turkey & Tomato Sauce

Serving Size: 4 | **Total Time:** 30 minutes

2 tbsp canola oil
1 lb ground turkey
1 egg
¼ cup bread crumbs
2 cloves garlic, minced
1 tsp dried oregano
1 tsp cumin
1 tsp red pepper flakes
Salt and pepper to taste
3 cups tomato sauce
8 oz rigatoni
2 tbsp grated Grana Padano

In a bowl, combine turkey, crumbs, cumin, garlic, and egg. Season with oregano, salt, red pepper flakes, and pepper. Form the mixture into meatballs. Warm the oil on Sauté in your Instant Pot. Cook the meatballs for 3-4 minutes until browned on all sides; set aside.

Add rigatoni to the cooker and pour the tomato sauce over. Cover with water. Stir well. Throw in the meatballs. Seal the lid and cook for 4 minutes on High Pressure. Release the pressure quickly. Serve topped with cheese.

Sunday Turkey Lettuce Wraps

Serving Size: 4 | **Total Time**: 35 minutes

¾ cup olive oil
4 cloves garlic, minced
3 tbsp maple syrup
2 tbsp pineapple juice
1 cup coconut milk
3 tbsp rice wine vinegar
3 tbsp soy sauce
1 tbsp Thai-style chili paste
1 lb turkey breast, boneless, cut into strips
1 lettuce, leaves separated
1/3 cup chopped peanuts
¼ cup chopped cilantro

In your Instant Pot, mix oil, garlic, rice wine vinegar, soy sauce, pineapple juice, maple syrup, coconut milk, and chili paste until smooth; add turkey strips and ensure they are submerged in the sauce. Seal the lid and cook on High Pressure for 12 minutes. Release the pressure quickly. Place the turkey at the center of each lettuce leaf. Top with cilantro and chopped peanuts.

Homemade Turkey Pepperoni Pizza

Serving Size: 4 | **Total Time**: 25 minutes

1 cup fire-roasted tomatoes, diced
1 cup turkey pepperoni, chopped
1 pizza crust
1 tsp oregano
7 oz gouda cheese, grated
2 tbsp olive oil

Grease a baking pan with oil. Line some parchment paper and place the pizza crust in it. Spread the fire-roasted tomatoes over the pizza crust and sprinkle with oregano. Make a layer with cheese and top with pepperoni. Add a trivet to your Instant Pot and pour in 1 cup water. Seal the lid and cook for 15 minutes on High Pressure. Do a quick release. Remove the pizza and serve.

Turkish-Style Roasted Turkey

Serving Size: 6 | **Total Time:** 70 minutes

2 lb boneless turkey breast, halved
2 garlic cloves, crushed
1 tsp dried basil
Salt and pepper to taste
3 whole cloves
½ cup soy sauce
½ cup lemon juice
¼ cup oil
3 cups chicken broth

Place the turkey in a Ziploc bag and add basil, cloves, soy sauce, oil, salt, pepper, and lemon juice. Pour in 1 cup of broth and seal. Shake and refrigerate for 30 minutes. Heat oil on Sauté in your Instant Pot. Cook the garlic for 2 minutes. Add in turkey and 2 tbsp of the marinade and the remaining broth. Seal the lid. Cook on Manual for 25 minutes on High. Release the pressure naturally. Serve.

Spicy Turkey Casserole with Tomatoes

Serving Size: 4 | **Total Time:** 30 minutes

2 (14-oz) cans fire-roasted tomatoes
2 bell peppers, cut into thick strips
2 tbsp olive oil
½ sweet onion, diced
3 cloves garlic, minced
1 jalapeño pepper, minced
1 lb turkey breast, cubed
1 cup salsa
2 tsp chili powder
1 tsp ground cumin
Salt to taste
1 tbsp oregano, chopped

Warm oil on Sauté. Add in garlic, onion, and jalapeño and cook for 5 minutes until fragrant. Stir in turkey and cook for 5-6 minutes until browned. Add in salsa, tomatoes, bell peppers, and 1 ½ cups water. Season with salt, cumin, and chili powder. Seal the lid, press Manual, and cook for 10 minutes on High. Release the pressure quickly. Top with oregano and serve.

Cranberry Turkey with Hazelnuts

Serving Size: 4 | **Total Time:** 40 minutes
1 lb turkey breasts, sliced
3 tbsp butter, softened
2 cups fresh cranberries
1 cup hazelnuts, chopped
1 cup red wine
1 tbsp rosemary, chopped
2 tbsp olive oil
2 tbsp orange zest
Salt and pepper to taste

Rub the turkey with oil and sprinkle with orange zest, salt, pepper, and rosemary. Melt butter in your Instant Pot on Sauté and brown turkey breast for 5-6 minutes. Pour in the wine, cranberries, and 1 cup of water. Seal the lid. Cook on High Pressure for 25 minutes. Do a quick release. Serve with chopped hazelnuts.

Parsley & Lemon Turkey Risotto

Serving Size: 4 | **Total Time:** 40 minutes
2 boneless turkey breasts, cut into strips
2 lemons, zested and juiced
1 tbsp dried oregano
2 garlic cloves, minced
1 ½ tbsp olive oil
1 onion, diced
2 cups chicken broth
1 cup arborio rice, rinsed
Salt and pepper to taste
¼ cup chopped parsley
8 lemon slices

In a Ziploc bag, mix turkey, oregano, salt, garlic, juice and zest of two lemons. Marinate for 10 minutes. Warm oil on Sauté in your Instant Pot. Add onion and cook for 3 minutes. Stir in the rice and chicken broth and season with pepper and salt.

Empty the Ziploc having the chicken and marinade into the pot. Seal the lid and cook on High Pressure for 12 minutes. Release the pressure quickly. Garnish with lemon slices and parsley to serve.

Sage Turkey & Red Wine Casserole

Serving Size: 4 | **Total Time**: 50 minutes
1 lb boneless turkey breast, cubed
1 onion, sliced
1 celery stalk, sliced
2 tbsp olive oil
1 carrot, diced
½ cup red wine
Salt and pepper to taste
1 cup chicken broth
1 tbsp tomato puree
2 tbsp sage, chopped

Warm olive oil in your IP on Sauté. Add in the turkey cubes and brown for 4-5 minutes, stirring occasionally; set aside. Add onion, celery, and carrot to the pot and sauté for 3-4 minutes. Stir in tomato puree, red wine, salt, and pepper and pour in chicken broth. Stir and return the turkey. Seal the lid, select Manual, and cook for 20 minutes on High. Once ready, release pressure naturally for 10 minutes. Unlock the lid, top with sage and serve.

Spicy Ground Turkey Chili with Vegetables

Serving Size: 6 | **Total Time**: 60 minutes
1 tbsp olive oil
1 small onion, diced
2 garlic cloves, minced
1 lb ground turkey
2 bell peppers, chopped
6 potatoes, chopped
1 cup carrots, chopped
1 cup corn kernels, roasted
1 cup tomato puree
1 cup diced tomatoes
1 cup chicken broth
1 tbsp ground cumin
1 tbsp chili powder
Salt and pepper to taste

Warm oil on Sauté in your Instant Pot and stir-fry onion and garlic until soft for about 3 minutes. Stir in turkey and cook until thoroughly browned, about 5-6 minutes. Add the bell peppers, potatoes, carrots, corn, tomato puree, tomatoes, broth, cumin, chili powder, salt, and pepper, and stir to combine. Seal the lid and cook for 25 minutes on High Pressure. Do a quick release. Set to Sauté and cook uncovered for 15 more minutes. Serve.

Turkey & Black Bean Chili

Serving Size: 6 | **Total Time:** 30 minutes

2 lb chopped turkey breast
1 ½ cups vegetable stock
2 (14-oz) cans black beans
2 garlic cloves, peeled
1 onion, diced
1 yellow bell pepper, diced
1 (7 oz) green chiles, diced
1 (14 oz) can diced tomatoes
1 tbsp hot sauce
½ tsp cumin
½ tbsp chili powder
1 cup cheddar, shredded

Place turkey, vegetable stock, black beans, garlic, onion, bell pepper, tomatoes, chiles, cumin, hot sauce, and chili powder in your Instant Pot and stir. Seal the lid, select Manual, and cook for 20 minutes on High pressure. Once done, allow a natural release for 10 minutes, then a quick pressure release, and unlock the lid. Top with cheddar and serve.

Turkey Stew with Salsa Verde

Serving Size: 4 | **Total Time:** 52 minutes

1 lb turkey thighs, boneless and diced
2 tbsp olive oil
1 cup pearl onions
1 carrot, julienned
1 cup green peas
1 cup salsa verde
Salt and pepper to taste
¼ tsp turmeric
¼ tsp cumin

Warm olive oil in your IP on Sauté. Add in the turkey pieces and brown for 4-5 minutes, stirring occasionally; set aside. Add pearl onions and carrot to the pot and sauté for 3-4 minutes. Stir in the turmeric, cumin, salt, and pepper and pour in 1 cup of water. Return the turkey.

Seal the lid, select Manual, and cook for 20 minutes on High. Once ready, allow a natural pressure release for 10 minutes. Unlock the lid, add in the green peas and salsa verde, and stir. Press Sauté and cook for 3 minutes.

Potato Skins with Shredded Turkey

Serving Size: 4 | **Total Time:** 30 minutes

2 cups vegetable broth
1 tsp chili powder
1 tsp ground cumin
½ tsp onion powder
½ tsp garlic powder
1 lb turkey breast
4 potatoes
1 Fresno chili, minced
Salt and pepper to taste

In the pot, combine broth, cumin, garlic powder, onion powder, and chili powder. Toss in turkey to coat. Place a steamer rack over the turkey. On top of the rack, set the steamer basket. Use a fork to pierce the potatoes and transfer to the steamer basket. Seal the lid and cook for 20 minutes on High. Release the pressure quickly.

Remove rack and steamer basket from the cooker. Shred the turkey in a bowl. Place the potatoes on a plate. Cut in half each potato lengthwise and scoop out the insides. Season with salt and pepper. Stuff with shredded turkey. Top with chili pepper.

Turkey Soup with Noodle

Serving Size: 6 | **Total Time:** 40 minutes

1 tbsp olive oil
1 onion, minced
3 cloves garlic, minced
1 turnip, chopped
1 cup celery rib, chopped
1 tbsp dry basil
1 bay leaf
6 cups vegetable broth
1 lb turkey breasts, cubed
8 oz dry egg noodles
Salt and pepper to taste

Warm olive oil on Sauté. Stir-fry in garlic and onion for 3 minutes. Mix in celery, bay leaf, basil, and turnip. Pour in 3 cups of broth. Scrape any brown bits from the pan's bottom and add turkey. Seal the lid and cook on High Pressure for 10 minutes. Naturally release the pressure. Transfer turkey breasts to another bowl.

Do away with the skin and bones. Using two forks, shred the meat. Set the cooker on Sauté. Transfer the turkey to the pot; add noodles and the remaining broth. Simmer for 10 minutes until noodles are done. Season and serve.

Caribbean Turkey Wings

Serving Size: 4 | **Total Time**: 55 minutes

- 2 lb turkey wings
- 2 tbsp vegetable oil
- 2 tbsp butter
- Salt and pepper to taste
- 1 yellow onion, sliced
- ½ cup brown sugar
- 1 tbsp bonnet pepper sauce
- ¼ cup chives, chopped
- 1 cup pineapple juice
- 1 tbsp cornstarch

Warm the vegetable oil and butter in your Instant Pot on Sauté. Sprinkle turkey wings with salt and pepper and place them in the pot. Sear for 5-6 minutes on all sides; set aside. Place onion in the pot and cook for 2 minutes. Stir in pineapple juice, bonnet pepper sauce, brown sugar, and 1/2 cup of water. Put in turkey wings and seal the lid. Select Manual and cook for 20 minutes on High.

When done, allow a natural release for 10 minutes and unlock the lid. Remove wings to a plate. Mix cornstarch and some cooking liquid in a bowl and pour into the pot. Simmer for 5 minutes on Sauté until the sauce thickens. Top with chives and serve with sauce.

Turkey Meatball Soup with Rice

Serving Size: 4 | **Total Time:** 30 minutes

1 green bell pepper, chopped
1 habanero pepper, seeded and minced
2 tbsp olive oil
1 onion, chopped
2 garlic cloves, minced
½ lb ground turkey
1 carrot, chopped
1 (14-oz) can diced tomatoes
½ tsp cumin
½ tsp oregano
½ cup white rice, rinsed
Salt and pepper to taste
1 egg, beaten
1 cup yogurt

Mix ground turkey with cumin, oregano, salt, and pepper in a bowl. Shape the mixture into 1-inch balls. Warm olive oil in your Instant Pot on Sauté. Add in onion, bell pepper, habanero pepper, carrot, and garlic. Cook for 3-4 minutes. Add in meatballs, tomatoes, 3 cups water, and rice. Seal the lid, select Manual and cook for 15 minutes.

Once ready, perform a quick pressure release and unlock the lid. Mix the egg and yogurt in a bowl, and temper with one cup of the soup liquid, adding it slowly and whisking constantly to prevent the egg from cooking. Stir this mixture into the pot. Ladle the soup into bowls and serve immediately.

Hungarian-Style Turkey Stew

Serving Size: 4 | **Total Time:** 40 minutes

1 lb chopped turkey pieces
2 tbsp butter
1 tsp paprika
1 can (15 oz) diced tomatoes
1 red onion, sliced
2 garlic cloves, chopped
1 red bell pepper, chopped
1 green bell pepper, chopped
1 cup chicken stock
Salt and pepper to taste
6 tbsp sour cream
2 tbsp parsley, chopped

Melt butter in your Instant Pot on Sauté and cook the turkey for 5 minutes, stirring occasionally. Add in onion, garlic, and bell peppers and sauté for another 3 minutes. Stir in paprika, tomatoes, and stock and seal the lid. Select Manual and cook for 20 minutes on High pressure. Once over, perform a quick pressure release and unlock the lid. Adjust the seasoning. Top with sour cream and parsley.

Buffalo Turkey Chili

Serving Size: 4 | **Total Time:** 40 minutes

1 lb ground turkey
2 tbsp olive oil
1 onion, diced
½ habanero pepper, diced
½ cup red bell pepper, diced
1 (14 oz) can pinto beans
½ cup hot Buffalo sauce
2 ½ cups chicken stock
1 tsp oregano
1 tbsp chili powder
Salt and pepper to taste
2 tbsp cilantro, chopped

Warm the olive oil in your Instant Pot on Sauté and cook the onion, habanero pepper, and bell pepper until tender, about 3-4 minutes. Stir in ground turkey, beans, chicken stock, buffalo sauce, oregano, chili powder, salt, and pepper. Seal the lid and cook for 15 minutes on Bean/Chili on High pressure. When over, allow a natural release for 10 minutes, then perform a quick pressure release and unlock the lid. Serve topped with cilantro.

Turkey Sausage with Brussels Sprouts

Serving Size: 4 | **Total Time:** 40 minutes

1 lb turkey sausage, sliced
2 tbsp olive oil
1 yellow onion, chopped
2 garlic cloves, minced
½ lb Brussels sprouts, sliced
¼ cup chicken broth
1 tsp yellow mustard
1 tsp balsamic vinegar
Salt and pepper to taste

Warm the olive oil in your Instant Pot on Sauté. Place in onion and garlic and cook for 2 minutes. Add in turkey sausage and cook for 5 more minutes. Stir in Brussels sprouts, mustard, vinegar, salt, and pepper for 3 minutes. Pour in chicken broth. Seal the lid, select Manual, and cook for 15 minutes on High pressure. When ready, allow a natural release for 5 minutes, then a quick pressure release, and unlock the lid. Serve right away.

Potato & Cauliflower Turkey Soup

Serving Size: 4 | **Total Time:** 35 minutes

1 tbsp olive oil
1 lb ground turkey
2 garlic cloves, minced
1 leek, chopped
1 cup cauliflower florets
1 carrot, chopped
1 celery stalk, chopped
1 cup tomato sauce
½ tsp dried sage
½ tsp dried thyme
4 cups chicken broth
3 potatoes, chopped
Salt and pepper to taste

Warm the olive oil in your Instant Pot on Sauté. Place the ground turkey and garlic and cook for 5-6 minutes. Remove to a bowl. Add the leek, carrot, celery, cauliflower, tomato sauce, chicken broth, potatoes, sage, and thyme to the pot and return the turkey. Seal the lid, select Manual, and cook for 8 minutes on High. When over, allow a natural release for 10 minutes and unlock the lid. Sprinkle with salt and pepper. Serve right away.

North African Turkey Stew

Serving Size: 4 | **Total Time:** 60 minutes

1 lb turkey breast, cubed
2 tbsp butter
1 onion, diced
½ tsp garlic powder
2 tsp ras el hanout
1 carrot, sliced
2 celery stalks, chopped
15.5 oz chickpeas, drained
2 oz green olives, pitted
3 ½ cups chicken broth
Salt and pepper to taste
2 tbsp cilantro, chopped

Melt butter in your Instant Pot on Sauté and cook the onion, carrot, and celery for 3-4 minutes. Stir in turkey breast and cook until browned, about 4-5 minutes. Mix in garlic powder, ras el hanout, salt, pepper, chickpeas, and chicken broth. Seal the lid, select Manual, and cook for 25 minutes on High pressure. When done, allow a natural release for 10 minutes and unlock the lid. Serve topped with green olives and cilantro.

Weekend Turkey with Vegetables

Serving Size: 4 | **Total Time:** 35 minutes

1 lb turkey breast, chopped
1 tsp red pepper flakes
2 cups canned tomatoes
3 cups chicken broth
1 tsp honey
2 cups zucchini, cubed
3 garlic cloves, chopped
1 onion, finely chopped
2 tbsp tomato paste
1 cup baby carrots, chopped
Salt and pepper to taste
2 tbsp olive oil

Mix turkey, red pepper flakes, tomatoes, broth, honey, zucchini, garlic, onion, tomato paste, carrots, salt, pepper, and olive oil in your Instant Pot. Seal the lid and cook on Meat/Stew for 25 minutes on High Pressure. When ready, do a quick release and open the lid. Serve.

Turkey with Rice & Peas

Serving Size: 6 | **Total Time**: 45 minutes

1 ½ lb turkey breasts, sliced
1 tbsp olive oil
1 small onion, sliced
1 cup brown rice
1 cup green peas
2 cups chicken broth
Salt and pepper to taste

Warm the olive oil in your Instant Pot on Sauté. Add in the onion and turkey and cook for 3 minutes, stirring occasionally. Stir in rice for 1 minute and pour in the broth; season with salt and pepper. Seal the lid, select Manual, and cook for 20 minutes on High.

Once ready, allow a natural release for 10 minutes, then perform a quick pressure release and unlock the lid. Mix in green peas and cook for 3-4 minutes on Sauté. Serve.

Mediterranean Duck with Olives

Serving Size: 4 | **Total Time**: 20 minutes

½ cup sun-dried tomatoes, chopped
1 lb duck breasts, halved
2 tbsp olive oil
½ tbsp Italian seasoning
Salt and pepper to taste
2 garlic cloves, minced
½ cup chicken stock
¾ cup heavy cream
1 cup kale, chopped
½ cup Parmesan, grated
10 Kalamata olives, pitted

Combine olive oil, Italian seasoning, pepper, salt, and garlic in a bowl. Add in the duck breasts and toss to coat. Set your Instant Pot to Sauté. Place in duck breasts and cook for 5-6 minutes on both sides. Pour in chicken stock and seal the lid. Select Manual and cook for 4 minutes.

When done, perform a quick pressure release and unlock the lid. Mix in heavy cream, tomatoes, Kalamata olives, and kale and cook for 5 minutes on Sauté. Serve topped with Parmesan cheese.

Honey-Glazed Turkey

Serving Size: 4 | **Total Time**: 60 minutes

1 large turkey breast
½ cup honey
½ tsp cumin
½ tsp turmeric
Salt and pepper to taste
2 cups chicken stock
1 onion, diced
2 garlic cloves, minced
1 tbsp dry sherry

Combine honey, cumin, turmeric, salt, and pepper in a bowl. Rub the mixture onto the turkey and let sit for 10 minutes. Place onion, garlic, and turkey in your Instant Pot. Add in chicken stock and sherry. Seal the lid and cook for 30 minutes on Manual. When ready, allow a natural release for 10 minutes. Slice turkey before serving.

Roast Goose with White Wine

Serving Size: 4 | **Total Time**: 40 minutes

1 lb goose fillets, sliced
1 onion, chopped
4 tbsp butter, softened
2 garlic cloves, crushed
1 cup white wine
2 tbsp fresh celery, chopped
1 tsp dried thyme
Salt and pepper to taste

Season the goose with salt and white pepper. Melt butter on Sauté in your Instant Pot and stir-fry onions, celery, and garlic for 3-4 minutes. Add the goose fillets and brown on both sides for 6-8 minutes. Add in the white wine and thyme. Pour in 1 cup of water, seal the lid, and set to Meat/Stew. Cook for 25 minutes on High Pressure. When ready, do a quick release and set aside. Serve.

Duck Breasts with Honey-Mustard Glaze

Serving Size: 4 | **Total Time:** 50 minutes

- 1 lb duck breast
- 1 tbsp oil
- 1 tsp onion powder
- 1 cup honey
- ¼ cup soy sauce
- ¼ cup dry sherry
- 1 tbsp Dijon mustard
- 3 cups chicken broth
- **Salt and pepper to taste**

Rub the duck with onion powder, salt, and pepper. Place it in the Instant Pot. Pour the broth, seal the lid and cook on Meat/Stew for 35 minutes on High Pressure.

Do a quick release. Remove the duck. Heat oil on Sauté, add soy sauce, honey, sherry, and mustard. Stir well and cook for 3-4 minutes. Add the meat and coat well. Serve the meat topped with the sauce.

PORK

Awesome Pork & Celery Soup

Serving Size: 4 | **Total Time:** 45 minutes

1 ¼ lb pork ribs
1 leek, chopped
1 onion, chopped
1 cup celery root, diced
½ cup parsley, chopped
4 cups beef broth
1 tsp salt
1 tsp red chili flakes
2 bay leaves
A handful of basil, torn
2 tbsp olive oil

Heat oil on Sauté. Add the ribs in batches and brown on all sides for 5-6 minutes. Add leek, onion, celery, parsley, broth, salt, red chili flakes, bay leaves, and basil.

Seal the lid and cook on Meat/Stew on High for 30 minutes. Do a quick release. Serve.

Delicious Pork & Vegetables Soup

Serving Size: 4 | **Total Time:** 50 minutes

2 (8-oz) pork chops
1 tbsp cayenne pepper
1 tsp chili powder
½ tsp garlic powder
4 cups beef broth
2 tbsp olive oil
2 large carrots, chopped
2 celery stalks, diced
1 onion, diced
2 tbsp soy sauce

Warm the olive oil in your Instant Pot on Sauté and stir-fry the onion until translucent, 3 minutes. Add celery stalks, carrots, cayenne, and chili pepper. Give it a good stir and continue to cook for 6-7 minutes. Add in pork chops, garlic, and soy sauce.

Pour in the broth and seal the lid. Cook on Manual for 25 minutes on High. Do a quick release. Let chill for 5 minutes. Serve.

Cajun Orange Pork Shoulder

Serving Size: 6 | **Total Time:** 60 minutes + marinating time

3 lb pork shoulder, trimmed of excess fat
2 garlic cloves, sliced
1 tsp cumin
1 tsp Cajun seasoning
1 large onion, sliced
¼ cup lime juice
¼ cup orange juice
Salt and pepper to taste
2 tbsp olive oil
2 tbsp cilantro, chopped

Mix the cumin, Cajun seasoning, garlic, onion, lime juice, orange juice, salt, and pepper in a bowl. Place in the pork shoulder and toss to coat. Let sit covered in the fridge for 30 minutes. Warm the olive oil in your Instant Pot on Sauté. Place in pork shoulder and cook for 10 minutes on all sides. Set aside.

Pour the remaining marinade into the pot and scrape any brown bits from the bottom. Pour in 1 cup of water and fit in a trivet. Place the pork inside the trivet and seal the lid. Select Manual and cook for 30 minutes on High.

When over, allow a natural release for 10 minutes, then perform a quick pressure release, and unlock the lid. Remove and slice the pork. Top with cilantro. Serve.

Garlic & Thyme Pork

Serving Size: 4 | **Total Time:** 58 minutes

1 lb pork brisket
2 garlic cloves, minced
2 tsp paprika
1 tsp ground cumin
1 tsp onion powder
2 tbsp flour
2 tbsp olive oil
1 ½ cups chicken broth
½ cup red wine
6 garlic cloves, minced
1 tbsp thyme, chopped
1 tbsp butter
1 cup mushrooms, sliced
Salt and pepper to taste

Mix the onion powder, paprika, cumin, salt, pepper, and garlic in a bowl. Sprinkle pork brisket with this mixture. Cover all brisket with flour. Warm the oil in your Instant Pot on Sauté. Place in brisket and cook for 8 minutes on all sides. Pour in red wine and scrape any brown bits from the bottom. Add in garlic, thyme, and broth and seal the lid. Select Manual and cook for 30 minutes. When ready, allow a natural release for 10 minutes, then perform a quick pressure release, and unlock the lid. Remove brisket to a plate and cooking liquid in a bowl. Melt butter in your Instant Pot on Sauté. Place in mushrooms and cook until they are soft. Pour in reserved liquid and cook for another minute. Cut brisket in slices and top with mushroom sauce. Serve warm.

German-Style Red Cabbage with Apples

Serving Size: 4 | **Total Time:** 20 minutes

1 cup Granny Smith apples, cubed
1 head red cabbage, shredded
2 tbsp olive oil
4 oz bacon, chopped
1 sweet onion, chopped
2 garlic cloves, chopped
1 tbsp red wine vinegar
1 tsp ground cumin
Salt and pepper to taste

Warm olive oil in your Instant Pot on Sauté. Place the bacon, onion, and garlic and cook for 5 minutes.

Put in cabbage, vinegar, apples, cumin, salt, pepper, and 1 cup of water and seal the lid. Select Manual and cook for 10 minutes on High pressure. When done, perform a quick pressure release. Carefully unlock the lid. Adjust the taste with salt and pepper and serve.

Gruyere Mushroom & Mortadella Cups

Serving Size: 4 | **Total Time:** 20 minutes

4 eggs, beaten
1 tsp olive oil
½ tsp paprika
½ cup mushrooms, chopped
1 cup mortadella, chopped
1 tbsp parsley, minced
Salt and pepper to taste
2 tbsp Gruyere, grated

Mix the eggs, olive oil, 1 tbsp of water, and paprika in a bowl. Add in mushrooms, parsley, salt, pepper, and mortadella. Divide the mixture between ramekins and top with Gruyere cheese.

Pour 1 cup of water into your Instant Pot and fit in a trivet. Place the ramekins on the trivet and seal the lid. Select Manual and cook for 12 minutes on High pressure. Once ready, perform a quick pressure release. Carefully unlock the lid. Serve warm.

Asparagus Wrapped in Parma Ham

Serving Size: 4 | **Total Time**: 15 minutes

1 lb asparagus, trimmed
½ lb Parma ham, sliced
2 tbsp Parmesan, grated

Pour 1 cup of water into your Instant Pot and fit in a trivet. Wrap each asparagus spear with a ham slice and place on the trivet. Seal the lid, select Manual, and cook for 3 minutes on High pressure.

When over, allow a natural release for 5 minutes, then perform a quick pressure release, and unlock the lid. Transfer the wraps to a greased baking dish and sprinkle with the Parmesan cheese. Place under preheated broiler for about 4 minutes until the cheese is melted. Serve.

Ranch Potatoes with Ham

Serving Size: 4 | **Total Time**: 20 minutes

1 lb Yukon gold potatoes, quartered
4 oz cooked ham, chopped
1 tsp garlic powder
2 tsp chives, chopped
Salt to taste
1/3 cup Ranch dressing

Cover potatoes with salted water in your Instant Pot and seal the lid. Select Manual and cook for 7 minutes on High pressure.

When done, perform a quick pressure release and unlock the lid. Drain the potatoes and transfer to a bowl. Stir in ranch dressing, garlic powder, and ham. Sprinkle with chives and serve.

BEEF & LAMB

Easy Lamb & Spinach Soup

Serving Size: 5 | **Total Time**: 45 minutes
1 lb lamb shoulder, cubed
10 oz spinach, chopped
3 eggs, beaten
5 cups vegetable broth
3 tbsp olive oil
1 tsp salt

Place in your Instant Pot the lamb, spinach, eggs, broth, olive oil, and salt. Seal the lid, press Soup/Broth, and cook for 30 minutes on High Pressure. Do a natural pressure release for about 10 minutes. Serve warm.

Roast Lamb Leg with Potatoes

Serving Size: 6 | **Total Time**: 35 minutes
2 lb lamb leg
2 garlic cloves
1 tbsp thyme, chopped
1 lb potatoes
1 lemon, chopped
3 tbsp oil
¼ cup red wine vinegar
1 tsp brown sugar
1 tsp salt

Place the potatoes in the pot, and pour enough water to cover. Season with salt, add garlic, and seal the lid. Set to Meat/Stew. Cook for 20 minutes on High Pressure. Do a quick release and remove potatoes; reserve the liquid.

Rub the meat with oil and thyme. Place in the pot. Pour in red wine vinegar, sugar, and add lemon. Add 1 cup of the reserved liquid and seal the lid. Cook on High Pressure for 7 minutes. Do a quick release.

Lamb Shanks with Garlic & Thyme

Serving Size: 4 | **Total Time**: 65 minutes

2 ½ lb lamb shanks, trimmed of excess fat
Salt and pepper to taste
10 whole garlic cloves, peeled
1 cup vegetable broth
1 (14-oz) can diced tomatoes
1 onion, sliced
2 tbsp tomato paste
½ cup red wine
2 tbsp fresh thyme, chopped
2 tbsp butter
2 tsp balsamic vinegar

Sprinkle lamb shanks with salt and pepper. Warm the butter in your Instant Pot on Sauté. Place in lamb shanks and cook for 4-5 minutes on all sides until browned. Add in onion and garlic and sauté for 2 more minutes. Stir in vegetable broth, tomato paste, red wine, tomatoes, and thyme and seal the lid. Select Manual and cook for 35 minutes on High.

Once done, allow a natural release for 10 minutes and unlock the lid. Remove lamb to a plate. Stir the butter and balsamic vinegar in the pot and select Sauté; cook until the sauce thickens. Serve the lamb with sauce.

Lamb with Tomato & Green Peas

Serving Size: 4 | **Total Time**: 65 minutes

1 cup green peas
1 lb lamb, cubed
1 tomato, roughly chopped
1 onion, peeled, chopped
2 carrots, peeled, chopped
1 celery stalk, chopped
2 tbsp parsley, chopped
2 garlic cloves, crushed
4 tbsp tomato sauce
2 tbsp olive oil
4 cups vegetable stock
Salt and pepper to taste

Warm the olive oil in your Instant Pot on Sauté. Cook the onion, carrots, celery, and garlic for 8 minutes until tender. Add in the lamb and sauté for another 5-6 minutes. Season with salt and black pepper. Add in green peas, tomato, tomato sauce, and stock and seal the lid. Cook on High Pressure for 30 minutes. Do a natural pressure release for about 10 minutes. Carefully fully unlock the lid. Top with parsley to serve.

Minty Lamb

Serving Size: 6 | **Total Time:** 55 minutes

3 lb lamb, boneless and cubed
2 tbsp butter
4 garlic cloves, minced
4 green onions, chopped
1 tsp cumin seeds
1 tsp coriander seeds
3 tbsp flour
1 ½ cups vegetable stock
1 cup carrots, sliced
4 mint sprigs
Salt and pepper to taste

Sprinkle the lamb with salt and pepper and coat in flour. Melt butter in your Instant Pot on Sauté. Add in onion and garlic and cook for 3 minutes. Put in lamb and cook for 5-6 minutes until browned. Stir in stock, carrots, cumin and coriander seeds, and mint sprigs and seal the lid. Select Manual and cook for 25 minutes on High.

When ready, allow a natural release for 10 minutes. Carefully unlock the lid. Discard the mint sprigs. Top the lamb with sauce and serve warm.

Hot Paprika & Oregano Lamb

Serving Size: 4 | **Total Time**: 70 minutes + marinating time

1 lb lamb shoulder
1 tsp hot paprika
1 tsp oregano
1 tsp cumin
¼ tsp ground cinnamon
2 tbsp tomato puree
¼ cup red wine
¼ cup chicken stock
1 tbsp olive oil
½ cup water
2 tbsp butter
Salt and pepper to taste

Mix the oregano, hot paprika, salt, black pepper, cumin, and cinnamon in a bowl. Add in lamb and toss to coat. Cover and let marinate for 20-30 minutes. Warm the olive oil in your Instant Pot on Sauté. Place in lamb shoulder and brown for 5 minutes on all sides. Pour in red wine, chicken stock, tomato puree, butter, and ½ cup of water.

Seal the lid, select Manual, and cook for 45 minutes on High pressure. Once over, allow a natural release for 10 minutes, then perform a quick pressure release, and unlock the lid. Remove the lamb to a cutting board shred it. Return to the pot and stir. Serve warm.

Mediterranean Lamb

Serving Size: 4 | **Total Time:** 55 minutes

1 lb lamb meat, cut into strips
1 tsp vegetable oil
4 tomatoes, chopped
2 tbsp tomato paste
1 red bell pepper, sliced
2 garlic cloves, minced
1 yellow onion, chopped
1 carrot, sliced
2 thyme sprigs
½ cup dry white wine
10 black olives, sliced
Salt and pepper to taste
2 tbsp parsley, chopped

Warm oil in your Instant Pot on Sauté. Add in lamb and cook for 8 minutes on all sides. Stir in tomatoes, tomato paste, bell pepper, garlic, onion, carrots, salt, pepper and sauté for 5 more minutes. Pour in wine and enough water to cover everything. Add in thyme sprigs and olives. Seal the lid, select Manual, and cook for 30 minutes on High.

Once done, perform a quick pressure release and unlock the lid. Remove the lamb to a plate, discard bones and shred it. Put the shredded lamb back to the pot and stir parsley. Serve immediately.

Quick French-Style Lamb with Sesame

Serving Size: 4 | **Total Time:** 45 minutes

12 oz lamb, tender cuts, ½-inch thick
1 cup rice
1 cup green peas
3 tbsp sesame seeds
4 cups beef broth
1 tsp salt
½ tsp dried thyme
3 tbsp butter

Mix the meat in the pot with broth. Seal the lid and cook on High Pressure for 15 minutes. Do a quick release. Remove the meat but keep the liquid. Add rice and green peas. Season with salt and thyme. Stir well and top with the meat. Seal the lid and cook on Manual for 18 minutes on High. Do a quick release. Carefully unlock the lid. Stir in butter and sesame seeds. Serve immediately.

Lamb Stew with Lemon & Parsley

Serving Size: 4 | **Total Time**: 60 minutes

2 potatoes, cut into bite-sized pieces
1 lb lamb neck, boneless
2 large carrots, chopped
1 tomato, diced
1 red bell pepper, chopped
1 garlic head, whole
2 tbsp parsley, chopped
¼ cup lemon juice
Salt and pepper to taste

Add the meat and season with salt. Add in potatoes, carrots, tomato, bell pepper, lemon juice, and pepper, tuck in one garlic head in the middle of the pot and add 2 cups water. Add parsley and seal the lid. Cook on High Pressure for 45 minutes. When ready, do a quick release. Carefully unlock the lid. Serve.

Simple Roast Lamb

Serving Size: 4 | **Total Time**: 40 minutes

2 lb lamb leg
1 tbsp garlic powder
3 tbsp extra virgin olive oil
Salt and pepper to taste
4 rosemary sprigs, chopped

Grease the inner pot with oil. Rub the meat with salt, pepper, and garlic powder, and place in the Instant Pot. Pour enough water to cover and seal the lid. Cook on Meat/Stew for 30 minutes on High. Do a quick release. Make sure the meat is tender and falls off the bones. Top with cooking juices and rosemary. Serve.

Traditional Lamb with Vegetables

Serving Size: 6 | **Total Time:** 30 minutes

1 lb lamb chops, 1-inch thick
1 cup green peas, rinsed
3 carrots, chopped
3 onions, chopped
1 potato, chopped
1 tomato, chopped
3 tbsp olive oil
1 tbsp paprika
Salt and pepper to taste

Grease the Instant Pot with olive oil. Rub salt onto the lamb and make a bottom layer. Add peas, carrots, onions, potato, and tomato. Season with paprika. Add olive oil, 1 cup of water, salt, and pepper. Give it a good stir and seal the lid. Cook on Meat/Stew for 20 minutes on High Pressure. When ready, do a natural pressure release. Carefully unlock the lid. Serve hot.

Garlic Lamb with Thyme

Serving Size: 4 | **Total Time:** 60 minutes

2 lb lamb, cubed
2 garlic cloves, minced
1 cup onions, chopped
1 cup red wine
2 cups beef stock
2 tbsp butter, softened
2 celery stalks, chopped
1 tbsp fresh thyme
2 tbsp flour
Salt and pepper to taste

Rub the lamb with salt and pepper. Melt butter on Sauté and cook onions, celery, and garlic for 5 minutes. Add lamb and fry until browned for about 5-6 minutes. Dust the flour and stir. Pour in the stock and red wine. Seal the lid, and cook on High Pressure for 30 minutes. Do a natural release for 10 minutes. Serve with thyme.

Leg of Lamb with Garlic and Pancetta

Serving Size: 6 | **Total Time**: 40 minutes

2 lb lamb leg
6 garlic cloves
1 large onion, chopped
6 pancetta slices
1 tsp rosemary
Salt and pepper to taste
2 tbsp oil
3 cups beef broth

Heat the oil in your Instant Pot on Sauté. Add the pancetta and onion, making two layers. Season with salt and pepper and cook for 3 minutes until lightly browned.

Place the lamb on a separate dish. Using a sharp knife, make 6 incisions into the meat and place a garlic clove in each. Rub the meat with rosemary and transfer to the pot. Press Cancel and pour in the beef broth. Seal the lid and cook on High Pressure for 25 minutes. When done, do a natural pressure release. Serve.

Savory Irish Lamb Stew

Serving Size: 4 | **Total Time**: 36 minutes

1 lb lamb, cut into pieces
1 ½ tbsp canola oil
1 onion, sliced
2 tbsp cornstarch
2 potatoes, cubed
2 carrots, chopped
2 ½ cups beef broth
½ tsp dried oregano
Salt and pepper to taste

Season the lamb with salt and pepper. Heat the canola oil in your Instant Pot on Sauté. Sear the lamb until browned on all sides, about 4-5 minutes. Add onion, potatoes, carrots, broth, and oregano, and stir. Seal the lid and cook on High Pressure for 18 minutes. When ready, do a quick pressure release. Whisk the cornstarch with a little bit of water and stir it into the stew. Cook on Sauté for 3 more minutes. Serve hot.

Asian-Style Lamb Curry

Serving Size: 4 | **Total Time:** 55 minutes + marinating time

1 ½ lb lamb stew meat, cubed
½ cup coconut milk
4 garlic cloves, minced
Juice of ½ lime
1-inch piece ginger, grated
Salt and pepper to taste
2 tbsp yellow curry paste
½ tsp turmeric
2 tbsp butter
1 tbsp soy sauce
14 oz canned tomatoes, diced
3 carrots, sliced
1 onion, diced
1 eggplant, diced
2 tbsp cilantro, chopped
2 cups basmati rice, cooked

Mix coconut milk, garlic, lime juice, ginger, salt, and pepper in a bowl. Add in lamb cubes and toss to coat. Let marinate for 30 minutes. Set your Instant Pot to Sauté. Melt butter and add onion, curry paste, turmeric, eggplant, and carrots and cook for 3-4 minutes. Stir in tomatoes, soy sauce, and 1 cup water.

Add in the marinated lamb with their juice and seal the lid. Select Manual and cook for 30 minutes on High pressure. Once ready, allow a natural release for 10 minutes, then perform a quick pressure release, and unlock the lid. Serve with the rice topped with cilantro.

Spicy Lamb & Bean Chili

Serving Size: 4 | **Total Time:** 53 minutes

1 cup chopped green chilies
1 cup cannellini beans, soaked
1 lb ground lamb
2 tbsp olive oil
1 onion, chopped
½ tbsp chili powder
½ tsp cayenne pepper
1 tsp cumin
1 tsp fennel seeds
1 (14-oz) can diced tomatoes
1 tbsp tomato paste
3 cups chicken broth
Salt and pepper to taste

Warm the olive oil in your Instant Pot on Sauté. Add in ground lamb and cook for 5 minutes until mostly brown. Stir in onion, chili powder, cayenne pepper, cumin, fennel seeds, salt, and pepper and sauté for 3 minutes.

Pour in tomatoes, tomato paste, green chilies, cannellini beans, and chicken broth and seal the lid. Select Manual and cook for 25 minutes on High.

When ready, allow a natural release for 10 minutes and unlock the lid. Serve with sour cream.

Fennel Lamb Ribs

Serving Size: 4 | **Total Time:** 47 minutes

3 lb lamb ribs
2 tbsp olive oil
4 garlic cloves, chopped
3 tbsp all-purpose flour
1 ½ cups vegetable stock
½ tsp cumin
½ fennel bulb, sliced
2 carrots, chopped
4 rosemary sprigs
Salt and pepper to taste

Warm olive oil in your Instant Pot on Sauté. Sprinkle lamb ribs with salt and pepper and add them to the pot. Cook for 6-7 minutes on all sides. Add in garlic, cumin and fennel and cook for 3 more minutes. Stir in flour, stock, rosemary, and carrots and seal the lid. Select Manual and cook for 22 minutes on High. When ready, allow a natural release for 5 minutes and unlock the lid. Remove rosemary sprigs. Serve the ribs with sauce.

Lamb Chops with Mashed Potatoes

Serving Size: 6 | **Total Time:** 20 minutes

8 lamb chops
Salt to taste
3 sprigs rosemary, chopped
3 tbsp butter, softened
2 tbsp olive oil
1 tbsp tomato puree
1 green onion, chopped
1 cup beef stock
5 potatoes, peeled, chopped
1/3 cup milk
2 tbsp cilantro, chopped

Rub rosemary leaves and salt to the lamb chops. Warm oil and 2 tbsp of butter on Sauté. Brown lamb chops for 1 minute per each side; set aside. In the pot, mix tomato puree and green onion and cook for 2-3 minutes. Add the stock into the pot to deglaze and scrape the bottom to get rid of any browned food bits. Return the lamb chops to the pot. Set a steamer rack on lamb chops. Place the steamer basket on the rack. Pour in the potatoes.

Seal the lid and cook on High Pressure for 4 minutes. Release the pressure quickly. Remove trivet and steamer basket.

In a blender, add potatoes, milk, salt, and remaining butter. Blend well until you obtain a smooth consistency. Place the potato mash on a serving dish. Lay lamb chops on the mash. Drizzle with cooking liquid and top with cilantro.

Vegetable & Lamb Casserole

Serving Size: 4 | **Total Time**: 50 minutes

1 lb lamb stew meat, cubed
2 tbsp olive oil
1 onion, chopped
3 garlic cloves, minced
2 tomatoes, chopped
½ lb baby potatoes
½ lb green beans, chopped
1 carrot, chopped
1 onion, chopped
1 celery stalk, chopped
2 tbsp white wine
2 cups lamb stock
1 tsp Hungarian paprika
1 tsp cumin, ground
¼ tsp oregano, dried
¼ tsp rosemary, dried
Salt and pepper to taste

Warm the olive oil in your Instant Pot on Sauté. Add in lamb cubes and cook for 5-6 minutes until no longer pink. Stir in onion and garlic and sauté for another 3 minutes. Pour in tomatoes, potatoes, green beans, carrot, onion, celery, white wine, lamb stock, paprika, cumin, oregano, rosemary, salt, and pepper and seal the lid. Select Manual and cook for 20 minutes on High pressure. When over, allow a natural release for 10 minutes and unlock the lid.

Balsamic Lamb

Serving Size: 4 | **Total Time:** 45 minutes

2 lb lamb shanks
2 tbsp sesame oil
2 garlic cloves, peeled
1 onion, chopped
1 cup vegetable broth
1 tbsp tomato paste
½ tsp thyme
¼ tsp dried dill weed
1 tbsp balsamic vinegar
1 tbsp butter

Warm sesame oil in your Instant Pot on Sauté. Place in onion and garlic and sauté for 3 minutes. Stir in broth, tomato paste, dill, and thyme. Add in the lamb and seal the lid. Select Manual and cook for 25 minutes on High.

When ready, allow a natural release for 5 minutes and unlock the lid. Remove the lamb to a bowl. Stir the balsamic vinegar and butter in the pot for 1-2 minutes until the butter melts. Serve the lamb with sauce.

Lamb Chorba

Serving Size: 4 | **Total Time:** 35 minutes

2 lb lamb shanks
2 tbsp olive oil
2 garlic cloves, peeled
1 onion, chopped
1 celery stalk, chopped
1 tomato, chopped
1 carrot, chopped
2 tbsp oregano, chopped
Salt and pepper to taste
4 cups vegetable broth
1 tbsp white wine vinegar

Warm the olive oil in your Instant Pot on Sauté. Place in the lamb, celery, onion, carrot, and garlic and sauté for 6 minutes. Stir in vegetable broth, tomato, salt, and pepper. Seal the lid. Select Manual and cook for 20 minutes. Release the pressure quickly. Drizzle with vinegar and sprinkle with oregano to serve.

FISH & SEAFOOD

Chinese Shrimp with Green Beans

Serving Size: 2 | Total Time: 20 minutes

1 tbsp sesame oil
1 lb shrimp, deveined
½ cup diced onion
2 cloves garlic, minced
1 carrot, cut into strips
½ lb green beans, chopped
2 cups vegetable stock
3 tbsp soy sauce
2 tbsp rice wine vinegar
10 oz lo mein egg noodles
½ tsp toasted sesame seeds
Sea Salt and pepper to taste

Warm oil on Sauté. Stir-fry the shrimp for 5 minutes; set aside. Add in garlic and onion and cook for 3 minutes until fragrant. Mix in soy sauce, carrot, stock, beans, and rice wine vinegar. Add in noodles and ensure they are covered. Season with pepper and salt. Seal the lid and cook on High Pressure for 5 minutes. Release the pressure quickly. Place the main in 2 plates. Add the reserved shrimp, sprinkle with sesame seeds, and serve.

Cheesy Shrimp Scampi

Serving Size: 4 | Total Time: 10 minutes

1 lb shrimp, deveined
2 tbsp olive oil
1 clove garlic, minced
1 tbsp tomato paste
10 oz canned tomatoes, diced
½ cup dry white wine
1 tsp red chili pepper
1 tbsp parsley, chopped
Salt and pepper to taste
1 cup Grana Padano, grated

Warm the olive oil in your Instant Pot on Sauté. Add in garlic and cook for 1 minute. Stir in shrimp, tomato paste, tomatoes, white wine, chili pepper, parsley, salt, pepper, and ¼ cup of water and seal the lid. Select Manual and cook for 3 minutes on High pressure. Once done, perform a quick pressure release and unlock the lid. Serve garnished with Grana Padano cheese.

Indian Prawn Curry

Serving Size: 4 | **Total Time:** 30 minutes

1 ½ lb prawns, deveined
2 tbsp ghee
2 garlic cloves, minced
1 onion, chopped
1 tsp ginger, grated
½ tsp ground turmeric
1 tsp red chili powder
2 tsp ground cumin
2 tsp ground coriander
2 tbsp curry paste
2 cups coconut milk
1 cup tomatoes, chopped
2 habanero peppers, minced
Salt and pepper to taste
1 tbsp fresh lemon juice

Melt the ghee in your Instant Pot on Sauté. Add in garlic, onion, and ginger and cook for 4 minutes. Stir in the turmeric, chili powder, cumin, coriander, and curry paste and cook for 1 more minute. Stir in coconut milk, prawns, tomatoes, habanero peppers, salt, and pepper.

Seal the lid. Select Manual and cook for 5 minutes on Low. Once ready, allow a natural release for 10 minutes, then perform a quick pressure release, and unlock the lid. Top with lemon juice and serve.

Butter & Wine Lobster Tails

Serving Size: 4 | **Total Time:** 10 minutes

1 lb lobster tails, cut in half
½ cup white wine
½ cup butter, melted
1 tsp red pepper flakes

Pour ½ cup of water and white wine in your Instant Pot and fit in a trivet. Place lobster tails on the trivet and seal the lid. Select Steam and cook for 5 minutes on Low. When ready, perform a quick pressure release. Drizzle with butter and top with red pepper flakes to serve.

Ginger & Garlic Crab

Serving Size: 4 | **Total Time**: 15 minutes

1 lb crabs, halved
2 tbsp butter
1 shallot, chopped
1 garlic cloves, minced
1 cup coconut milk
1-inch ginger, sliced
1 lemongrass stalk
Salt and pepper to taste
1 lemon, sliced

Melt the butter in your Instant Pot on Sauté. Place in shallot, garlic, and ginger and cook for 3 minutes. Pour in coconut milk, crabs, lemongrass, salt, and pepper and seal the lid. Select Manual and cook for 6 minutes on High pressure. Once ready, perform a quick pressure release and unlock the lid. Serve with lemon slices.

Herby Crab Legs with Lemon

Serving Size: 4 | **Total Time**: 10 minutes

3 lb king crab legs, broken in half
1 tsp rosemary
1 tsp thyme
1 tsp dill
¼ cup butter, melted
Salt and pepper to taste
1 lemon, cut into wedges

Pour 1 cup of water into your Instant Pot and fit in a trivet. Season the crab legs with rosemary, thyme, dill, salt, and pepper; place on the trivet. Seal the lid, select Manual, and cook for 3 minutes. When ready, perform a quick pressure release. Remove crab legs to a bowl and drizzle with melted butter. Serve with lemon wedges.

Black Squid Ink Tagliatelle

Serving Size: 4 | **Total Time:** 25 minutes
18 oz squid ink tagliatelle, cooked
1 lb fresh seafood mix
¼ cup olive oil
4 garlic cloves, crushed
1 tbsp parsley, chopped
1 tsp rosemary, chopped
½ tbsp white wine

Heat 3 tbsp olive oil on Sauté and stir-fry the garlic for 1-2 minutes until fragrant. Add seafood, parsley, and rosemary and stir. Add the remaining oil, wine, and ½ cup of water. Seal the lid and cook on High Pressure for 4 minutes. Do a quick release and set aside. Open the lid, add the pasta, and stir. Serve hot.

Crab Pilaf with Broccoli & Asparagus

Serving Size: 4 | **Total Time:** 30 minutes
½ lb asparagus, trimmed and cut into 1-inch pieces
½ lb broccoli florets
Salt to taste
2 tbsp olive oil
1 small onion, chopped
1 cup rice
1/3 cup white wine
2 cups vegetable stock
8 oz lump crabmeat

Heat oil on Sauté and cook the onion for 3 minutes until soft. Stir in rice and cook for 1 minute. Pour in the wine. Cook for 2 to 3 minutes, stirring until the liquid has almost evaporated. Add vegetable stock and salt; stir.

Place a trivet on top. Arrange the broccoli and asparagus on the trivet. Seal the lid and cook on High Pressure for 8 minutes. Do a quick release. Remove the vegetables to a bowl. Fluff the rice with a fork and add in the crabmeat, heat for a minute. Taste and adjust the seasoning. Serve immediately topped with broccoli and asparagus.

Red Wine Squid

Serving Size: 4 | **Total Time:** 25 minutes

2 lb squid, chopped
2 tbsp olive oil
Salt and pepper to taste
½ cup red wine
½ fennel bulb, sliced
28 oz can crushed tomatoes
1 red onion, sliced
2 garlic cloves, minced
1 tsp Italian seasoning
½ cup parsley, chopped

Mix the olive oil, squid, salt, and pepper in a bowl. Pour the red wine, tomatoes, onion, garlic, Italian seasoning, and fennel in your Instant Pot and fit in a steamer basket. Put in the squid and seal the lid. Select Manual and cook for 4 minutes on High pressure. When ready, allow a natural release for 10 minutes, then perform a quick pressure release. Serve scattered with parsley.

White Wine Marinated Squid Rings

Serving Size: 3 | **Total Time:** 25 minutes + cooling time

1 lb fresh squid rings
1 cup dry white wine
1 cup olive oil
2 garlic cloves, crushed
1 lemon, juiced
2 cups fish stock
¼ tsp red pepper flakes
¼ tsp dried oregano
1 tbsp rosemary, chopped
1 tsp sea salt

In a bowl, mix wine, olive oil, lemon juice, garlic, flakes, oregano, rosemary, and salt. Submerge squid rings in this mixture and cover with a lid. Refrigerate for 1 hour. Remove the squid from the fridge and place it in the pot along with stock and half of the marinade. Seal the lid. Cook on High Pressure for 6 minutes. Release the pressure naturally for 10 minutes. Transfer the rings to a plate and drizzle with some marinade to serve.

Mussels With Lemon & White Wine

Serving Size: 5 | **Total Time:** 10 minutes

2 lb mussels, cleaned and debearded
1 cup white wine
½ cup water
1 tsp garlic powder
Juice from 1 lemon

In the pot, mix garlic powder, water, and wine. Put the mussels into the steamer basket; rounded-side should be placed facing upwards to fit as many as possible.

Insert a rack into the cooker and lower the steamer basket onto the rack. Seal the lid and cook on Low Pressure for 1 minute. Release the pressure quickly. Remove unopened mussels. Coat the mussels with the wine mixture and lemon juice and serve.

Chili Squid

Serving Size: 4 | **Total Time:** 35 minutes

1 lb squid, sliced into rings
1 tsp onion powder
2 tbsp flour
1 garlic clove, minced
1 tbsp chives
¼ tsp chili pepper, chopped
¼ tsp smoked paprika
1 tbsp lemon juice
1 cup vegetable broth
2 tbsp butter
Salt and pepper to taste
2 tbsp parsley, chopped

Mix the onion powder, smoked paprika, flour, garlic, chives, chili pepper, salt, and pepper in a bowl. Add in the squid slices and toss to coat. Let sit for 10 minutes.

Melt the butter in your Instant Pot on Sauté. Place in the squid mixture and cook for 3-4 minutes. Pour in the vegetable broth and seal the lid. Cook on Manual for 12 minutes on High. Once done, perform a quick pressure release and unlock the lid. Serve sprinkled with parsley.

Spicy Mussels & Anchovies with Rice

Serving Size: 4 | **Total Time**: 40 minutes

1 cup rice
6 oz mussels
1 onion, finely chopped
1 garlic clove, crushed
1 tbsp dried rosemary
¼ cup capers
Salt and chili pepper to taste
3 tbsp olive oil
4 salted anchovies

Add rice to the pot and pour 2 cups of water. Seal the lid and cook on Manual for 18 minutes on High. Do a quick release. Remove the rice and set aside. Grease the pot with oil, and stir-fry garlic and onion for 2 minutes on Sauté. Add mussels and rosemary. Cook for 10 more minutes. Stir in rice and season with salt and chili pepper. Serve with anchovies and capers.

Beer-Steamed Mussels

Serving Size: 4 | **Total Time**: 15 minutes

3 lb mussels, debearded
4 tbsp butter
1 shallot, chopped
2 garlic cloves, minced
2 tbsp parsley, chopped
1 cup beer
1 cup chicken stock

Melt butter in your Instant Pot on Sauté. Add in shallot and garlic and cook for 2 minutes. Stir in beer and cook for 1 minute. Mix in stock and mussels and seal the lid.

Select Manual and cook for 3 minutes on High pressure. Once ready, perform a quick pressure release. Discard unopened mussels. Serve sprinkled with parsley.

Basil Clams with Garlic & White Wine

Serving Size: 4 | **Total Time**: 15 minutes

1 lb clams, scrubbed
2 tbsp butter
4 green garlic, chopped
1 tbsp lemon juice
½ cup white wine
½ cup chicken stock
Salt and pepper to taste
2 tbsp basil, chopped

Melt the butter in your Instant Pot on Sauté. Add in the garlic and clams and cook for 3-4 minutes. Stir in lemon juice and chicken stock, white wine, salt, and pepper and seal the lid. Select Manual and cook for 3 minutes on High pressure. Once done, perform a quick pressure release and unlock the lid. Discard unopened clams. Serve topped with basil.

Saucy Clams with Herbs

Serving Size: 4 | **Total Time**: 15 minutes

1 lb clams, scrubbed
2 tsp olive oil
2 garlic cloves, minced
1 onion, chopped
2 celery stalks, diced
1 bell pepper, diced
1 tbsp tomato paste
28 oz can crushed tomatoes
½ tsp basil
1 tsp rosemary
½ tsp oregano
Salt and pepper to taste
¼ tsp chili pepper

Warm the olive oil in your Instant Pot on Sauté. Place in garlic, onion, celery, and bell pepper and cook for 3-4 minutes. Add in tomato paste and cook for another 1 minute. Stir in clams, tomatoes, basil, rosemary, oregano, salt, pepper, and chili pepper and seal the lid. Select Manual and cook for 2 minutes on High pressure. Once done, perform a quick pressure release and unlock the lid. Discard unopened clams. Serve with cooked rice.

Clam & Corn Chowder

Serving Size: 4 | **Total Time:** 30 minutes

2 tbsp olive oil
1 onion, chopped
3 potatoes, cubed
4 cups corn kernels
12 oz canned clams, chopped
1 green bell pepper, diced
1 red bell pepper, diced
Salt and pepper to taste
4 cups chicken broth
1 cup milk
1 tbsp flour
3 tbsp butter

Warm the olive oil in your Instant Pot on Sauté. Add in onion and bell peppers and cook for 3-4 minutes until tender. Stir in potatoes, corn kernels, clams with their juice, and chicken broth. Seal the lid, select Manual, and cook for 12 minutes on High. Once ready, perform a quick pressure release. Combine milk with flour and pour it into the pot. Press Sauté and stir in butter. Let simmer for 3-4 minutes.

Lime & Honey Scallops

Serving Size: 2 | **Total Time:** 15 minutes

1 lb sea scallops, shells removed
1 cup water
1 tbsp olive oil
3 tbsp honey
1 lime, juiced and zested
½ cup soy sauce
½ tsp ground ginger
½ tsp garlic powder
Salt to taste

Pour 1 cup of water into your Instant Pot and fit in a trivet. Place scallops, olive oil, honey, soy sauce, ginger, garlic powder, lime zest, and salt in a small pan and put it on the trivet. Seal the lid and cook for 6 minutes on Steam. Once ready, perform a quick pressure release and unlock the lid. Serve drizzled with lime juice.

Octopus & Shrimp with Collard Greens

Serving Size: 4 | **Total Time:** 30 minutes

6 oz octopus, cut into bite-sized pieces
1 lb collard greens, chopped
1 lb shrimp, whole
1 tomato, chopped
3 cups fish stock
4 tbsp olive oil
3 garlic cloves
2 tbsp parsley, chopped
1 tsp sea salt

Place shrimp and octopus in the pot. Add tomato and fish stock. Seal the lid and cook on High Pressure for 15 minutes. Do a quick release. Remove shrimp and octopus. Drain the liquid. Heat olive oil on Sauté and add garlic and parsley and cook for 1 minute. Add in collard greens, season with salt, and simmer for 5 minutes. Serve with shrimp and octopus.

Galician-Style Octopus

Serving Size: 6 | **Total Time:** 30 minutes

1 lb potatoes, sliced into rounds
2 lb whole octopus, cleaned and sliced
1 tbsp Spanish paprika
3 tbsp olive oil
Salt and pepper to taste

Place the potatoes in your Instant Pot and cover them with water. Place a trivet over the potatoes. Season the octopus with salt and pepper and place it onto the trivet. Seal the lid, select Manual, and cook for 15 minutes.

Once done, perform a quick pressure release and unlock the lid. Remove the octopus and let cool, then slice it into slices about half-inch thick. Transfer the sliced potatoes to a baking sheet and arrange octopus slices over the potatoes. Drizzle with olive oil and place under the broiler for 5 minutes. Sprinkle with paprika and serve.

White Wine Oysters

Serving Size: 4 | **Total Time**: 10 minutes

2 lb in-shell oysters, cleaned
1 cup vegetable broth
4 tbsp white wine
2 tbsp thyme, chopped
1 garlic clove, minced
Salt and pepper to taste
4 tbsp butter, melted

Place the vegetable broth, oysters, white wine, garlic, salt, and pepper in your Instant Pot and seal the lid. Select Manual and cook for 3 minutes on High pressure. Once done, perform a quick pressure release and unlock the lid. Drain the oysters, drizzle with the melted butter, and top with thyme to serve.

PASTA & RICE

Coconut Rice Breakfast

Serving Size: 4 | **Total Time**: 25 minutes

1 cup brown rice
1 cup water
1 cup coconut milk
½ cup coconut chips
¼ cup walnuts, chopped
¼ cup raisins
¼ tsp cinnamon powder
½ cup maple syrup

Place the rice and water in your Instant Pot. Seal the lid, select Manual, and cook for 15 minutes on High. When ready, perform a quick pressure release and unlock the lid. Stir in coconut milk, coconut chips, raisins, cinnamon, and maple syrup. Seal the lid, select Manual, and cook for another 5 minutes on High pressure. When over, perform a quick pressure release. Top with walnuts.

Prawn Basmati Rice

Serving Size: 4 | **Total Time**: 32 minutes

½ lb cooked prawns
¼ frozen peas
2 tbsp butter
1 cup basmati rice
1 ¼ cups water
Salt and pepper to taste

Place the rice, water, butter, and salt in your Instant Pot and stir. Seal the lid, select Manual, and cook for 6 minutes on High pressure. When ready, allow a natural release for 10 minutes and unlock the lid. Using a fork, fluff the rice and mix in prawns, peas, salt, and pepper. Let sit for 5-6 minutes until heated through. Serve.

Pomegranate Rice with Vegetables

Serving Size: 4 | **Total Time**: 15 minutes

¼ cup pomegranate seeds
2 tbsp olive oil
1 onion, finely chopped
2 cloves garlic, minced
1 cup basmati rice
1 cup sweet corn, frozen
1 cup garden peas, frozen
¼ tsp salt
1 tsp turmeric powder
1 ¼ cups vegetable stock

Warm oil your Instant Pot on Sauté and add onion and garlic; cook for 3 minutes until fragrant. Stir in rice, corn, peas, salt, turmeric, and stock. Seal the lid, select Manual, and cook for 4 minutes on High pressure. When ready, perform a quick pressure release and unlock the lid. With a fork, fluff the rice. Top with pomegranate and serve.

Hazelnut Brown Rice Pilaf

Serving Size: 4 | **Total Time**: 45 minutes

¼ cup hazelnuts, toasted and chopped
2 tbsp olive oil
1 cup brown rice
2 cups vegetable broth
Salt and pepper to taste

Place the rice, vegetable broth, olive oil, pepper, and salt in your Instant Pot and stir. Seal the lid, select Manual, and cook for 25 minutes on High. Once ready, allow a natural release for 10 minutes and unlock the lid. Using a fork, fluff the rice. Top with hazelnuts and serve.

Vegetable Green Biryani

Serving Size: 6 | **Total Time:** 15 minutes

1 tbsp olive oil
2 cups basmati rice
3 tbsp butter
2 garlic cloves, minced
1 lb spinach, chopped
1 cup broccoli florets, chopped
Salt and pepper to taste
4 tbsp cilantro, chopped
4 cups vegetable broth

Warm olive oil in your Instant Pot on Sauté. Add in the rice, butter, and garlic and cook for 1-2 minutes. In a food processor, blend the spinach, broccoli, and cilantro. Pour vegetable broth and mixed greens in the pot and stir. Season with salt and pepper. Seal the lid and cook on Manual for 6 minutes on High. Once ready, perform a quick pressure release and unlock the lid. Divide between four serving bowls and serve.

Wild Rice Pilaf

Serving Size: 4 | **Total Time:** 20 minutes

1 cup wild rice
2 tbsp butter
Salt and pepper to taste
2 tbsp chives, chopped

Stir the rice, butter, 2 cups of water, salt, and pepper in your Instant Pot. Seal the lid, select Manual, and cook for 5 minutes on High pressure. When ready, allow a natural release for 10 minutes and unlock the lid. Using a fork, fluff the rice. Top with chives and serve.

Spicy Indian Rice

Serving Size: 4 | **Total Time**: 40 minutes

2 tbsp olive oil
2 garlic cloves, minced
2 shallots, chopped
1 cup basmati rice
½ cup carrots, chopped
2 tsp masala curry paste
1 tsp ginger paste
1 ½ cups chicken broth
1 cup frozen green beans
Salt and pepper to taste
2 tbsp cilantro, chopped

Warm olive oil in your Instant Pot to Sauté. Add in shallots, ginger, and garlic and cook until fragrant, about 3 minutes. Stir in rice, carrots, masala curry paste, chicken broth, green beans, salt, and pepper. Seal the lid and cook on Manual for 20 minutes on High. Once ready, allow a natural release for 10 minutes and unlock the lid. With a fork, fluff the rice. Scatter with cilantro and serve.

Pilau Brown Rice

Serving Size: 4 | **Total Time**: 20 minutes

2 tbsp olive oil
1 bay leaf
1 tsp cumin
1 cup basmati brown rice
Sea salt to taste
1 ¼ cups vegetable broth
½ tbsp turmeric
2 tbsp cilantro, chopped

Place the olive oil, bay leaf, cumin, rice, salt, vegetable broth, and turmeric in your Instant Pot and stir. Seal the lid and cook for 6 minutes on Multigrain.

When done, allow a natural release for 10 minutes and unlock the lid. Using a fork, fluff the rice. Transfer to a serving plate. Top with cilantro and serve.

Rice & Red Bean Pot

Serving Size: 4 | **Total Time:** 55 minutes

1 cup red beans, soaked
2 tbsp vegetable oil
½ cup rice
½ tbsp cayenne pepper
1 ½ cups vegetable broth
1 onion, diced
1 garlic clove, minced
1 red bell pepper, diced
1 stalk celery, diced
Salt and pepper to taste

Place beans in your Instant Pot with enough water to cover them by a couple of fingers. Seal the lid and cook for 25 minutes on High Pressure. Release the pressure quickly. Drain the beans and set aside.

Rinse and pat dry the inner pot. Add in oil and press Sauté. Add in onion and garlic and sauté for 3 minutes until soft. Add celery and bell pepper and cook for 2 minutes.

Add in the rice, reserved beans, vegetable broth. Stir in pepper, cayenne pepper, and salt. Seal the lid and cook for 15 minutes on High Pressure. Release the pressure quickly. Carefully unlock the lid. Serve warm.

Rice & Chicken Soup

Serving Size: 4 | **Total Time:** 35 minutes

1 lb chicken breasts, cubed
1 carrot, chopped
1 onion, chopped
¼ cup rice
1 potato, finely chopped
1 tsp cayenne pepper
2 tbsp olive oil
4 cups chicken broth

Heat the olive oil in your Instant Pot on Sauté. Cook the onion, carrot, and chicken for 5 minutes, stirring often. Add in rice, potato, cayenne pepper, and broth and stir. Seal the lid. Cook on Soup/Broth for 20 minutes. Do a quick pressure release. Carefully unlock the lid. Serve.

One-Pot Mexican Rice

Serving Size: 4 | **Total Time:** 35 minutes

2 tbsp olive oil
1 onion, diced
2 garlic cloves, sliced
1 cup long-grain white rice
2 cups chicken stock
1 tbsp chipotle chili paste
2 mixed peppers, sliced
1 cup salsa
Salt and pepper to taste
2 tbsp cilantro, chopped

Warm olive oil in your Instant Pot on Sauté and add in onion, garlic, and mixed peppers; cook for 2-3 minutes.

Add in rice and cook for another 1-2 minutes. Mix in stock, salsa, salt, and pepper. Seal the lid, select Manual, and cook for 10 minutes on High pressure.

When over, allow a natural release for 10 minutes and unlock the lid. Stir in the chipotle paste. Serve topped with cilantro. Enjoy!

BEANS & GRAINS

Apricot Steel Cut Oats

Serving Size: 2 | **Total Time:** 25 minutes
¾ cup dry apricots, soaked and chopped
1 tbsp butter
1 cup steel oats
A pinch of salt
2 tbsp white sugar
2 oz cream cheese, softened
1 tsp milk
1 tsp cinnamon
¼ cup brown sugar

Melt butter in your Instant Pot on Sauté. Stir in oats for 3 minutes. Add in salt and 3 ½ cups water. Seal the lid, select Manual, and cook for 10 minutes on High pressure.

When done, allow a natural release for 5 minutes and unlock the lid. Stir in apricots and set aside. In the meantime, combine white sugar with cream cheese and milk in a bowl. In a separate bowl, mix cinnamon and brown sugar. Divide oats between bowls. Top with cinnamon and cream cheese and serve.

Honey Oat & Pumpkin Granola

Serving Size: 4 | **Total Time:** 45 minutes
1 tbsp soft butter
1 cup steel-cut oats
1 cup pumpkin puree
3 cups water
2 tsp cinnamon
A pinch of salt
¼ cup clear honey
1 tsp pumpkin pie spice

Set your Instant Pot to Sauté and melt in the butter. Stir in oats and cook for 3 minutes. Add in pumpkin puree, water, cinnamon, salt, honey, and pumpkin spice and stir. Seal the lid, select Manual, and cook for 10 minutes on High. Once ready, allow a natural release for 10 minutes. Stir the granola and let sit for 10 minutes. Serve.

Kiwi Steel Cut Oatmeal

Serving Size: 4 | **Total Time**: 25 minutes

2 kiwi, mashed
2 cups steel cut oatmeal
¼ tsp nutmeg
1 tsp cinnamon
1 tsp vanilla
¼ tsp salt
½ cup hazelnuts, chopped
¼ cup honey

Place the kiwi, oats, 3 cups water, nutmeg, cinnamon, vanilla, and salt in your Instant Pot and stir to combine. Seal the lid and cook on Manual for 10 minutes on High. When done, allow a natural release for 10 minutes and unlock the lid. Mix in hazelnuts and honey and let chill.

Southern Cheese Grits

Serving Size: 6 | **Total Time**: 35 minutes

2 tbsp olive oil
1 cup stone-ground grits
2 cups vegetable broth
1 cup milk
4 oz cheddar, shredded
3 tbsp butter
Salt to taste

Set your Instant Pot to Sauté. Warm the olive oil, place in grits and cook for 3 minutes until fragrant. Stir in broth, milk, cheese, butter, and salt. Seal the lid, select Manual, and cook for 10 minutes on High. Once ready, allow a natural release for 15 minutes and unlock the lid. Serve.

Coconut Cherry Steel Cut Oats

Serving Size: 4 | **Total Time**: 20 minutes

1 cup cherries, pitted and halved
1 cup steel-cut oats
1 cup coconut milk
2 cups water
½ tsp vanilla extract

Place cherries, oats, milk, water, and vanilla extract in your Instant Pot. Seal the lid, select Manual, and cook for 3 minutes on High pressure. Once ready, allow a natural release for 10 minutes and unlock the lid. Serve.

Jamaican Cornmeal Porridge

Serving Size: 4 | **Total Time**: 25 minutes

1 cup cornmeal
1 cup coconut milk
½ tsp nutmeg, ground
1 tsp vanilla extract
½ cup condensed milk
1 mango, sliced

Combine 1 cup of water and cornmeal in a bowl and stir. Add 3 cups of water, coconut milk, vanilla, nutmeg, and cornmeal mixture in your Instant Pot. Seal the lid, select Manual, and cook for 6 minutes on High. Once over, allow a natural release for 10 minutes and unlock the lid. Stir in condensed milk. Top with mango and serve.

Cheesy Polenta with Sundried Tomatoes

Serving Size: 4 | **Total Time**: 25 minutes

1 cup sun-dried tomatoes, finely chopped
2 tbsp olive oil
1 cup onion, diced
2 cloves garlic, chopped
2 tsp fresh oregano, minced
2 tbsp fresh parsley, minced
1 tsp kosher salt
4 cups vegetable stock
¼ cup Parmesan, shredded
1 cup polenta

Warm olive oil in your Instant Pot on Sauté and add in onion and garlic. Cook for 3 minutes until fragrant. Stir in tomatoes, oregano, parsley, salt, and stock. Top with polenta. Seal the lid, select Manual, and cook for 5 minutes on High pressure. When done, allow a natural release for 10 minutes. Top with Parmesan and serve.

Garlic Mushroom Polenta

Serving Size: 4 | **Total Time:** 35 minutes

1 cup mixed mushrooms, sliced
2 tsp olive oil
4 green onions, chopped
2 garlic cloves, sliced
2 tbsp cilantro, minced
1 tbsp chili powder
½ tsp cumin
Salt and pepper to taste
¼ tsp cayenne pepper
2 cups veggie stock
1 cup polenta

Warm olive oil in your Instant Pot on Sauté and add mushrooms, garlic, and green onions. Cook for 4 minutes. Stir in chili powder, cumin, salt, pepper, cayenne, and stock. Combine polenta with 1 ½ cups of hot water in a bowl and transfer to the Instant Pot. Seal the lid, select Manual, and cook for 10 minutes on High pressure. Once done, allow a natural release for 10 minutes and unlock the lid. Top with cilantro and serve.

APPETIZERS & SIDE DISHES

Potatoes & Tuna Salad with Pickles

Serving Size: 4 | **Total Time:** 15 minutes

½ cup pimento-stuffed green olives
½ cup chopped roasted red peppers
1 lb potatoes, quartered
2 eggs
3 tbsp melted butter
Salt and pepper to taste
6 pickles, chopped
2 tbsp red wine vinegar
10 oz canned tuna, drained

Pour 2 cups of water into the pot and add potatoes. Place a trivet over the potatoes. Lay the eggs on the trivet. Seal the lid and cook for 8 minutes on High Pressure. Do a quick release. Drain and remove potatoes to a bowl.

Fill a bowl with ice water. Add in the eggs to cool. Drizzle melted butter over the potatoes and season with salt and pepper. Peel and chop the chilled eggs. Add pickles, eggs, peppers, tuna, and red wine vinegar to the potatoes and mix to coat. Serve topped with olives. Enjoy!

Grandma's Egg Salad

Serving Size: 6 | **Total Time:** 15 minutes

6 eggs
¼ cup crème frâiche
2 spring onions, minced
1 tbsp dill, minced
1 tbsp curry paste
2 tsp mustard
Salt and pepper to taste

Grease a cake pan with cooking spray. Carefully crack in the eggs. To the inner pot, add 1 cup water and a trivet. Set the pan with the eggs on the trivet. Seal the lid and cook for 5 minutes on High Pressure. When ready, do a quick release. Drain any water from the eggs in the pan.

Loosen the eggs on the edges with a knife. Transfer to a cutting board and chop into smaller sizes. Transfer the chopped eggs to a bowl. Add in onions, mustard, salt, dill, crème frâiche, curry paste, and pepper. Serve.

Arugula Salad with Sweet Potatoes & Eggs

Serving Size: 4 | **Total Time**: 20 minutes

4 sweet potatoes, peeled and diced
2 large eggs
2 ½ cups mayonnaise
¼ cup dill, chopped
1/3 cup Greek yogurt
½ cup arugula

Pour 1 cup of water into the Instant Pot and insert a steamer basket. Place in the eggs and potatoes. Seal the lid. Cook for 4 minutes on High Pressure. When ready, do a quick release. Take out the eggs and place in a bowl of ice-cold water for purposes of cooling. In a bowl, mix yogurt, mayonnaise, and dill. In a separate bowl, mash potatoes using a potato masher. Coat them with the mayonnaise mixture. Skin and dice the eggs. Add them to the potato salad and mix. Serve with arugula.

Authentic German Salad with Bacon

Serving Size: 6 | **Total Time**: 20 minutes

6 smoked bacon slices, chopped
6 red potatoes, peeled and quartered
½ cup apple cider vinegar
2 tsp mustard
Salt and pepper to serve
2 red onions, chopped

Set your Instant Pot to Sauté. Briefly brown the bacon for 5 minutes until crispy. Set aside. In a bowl, mix mustard, vinegar, ½ cup water, salt, and pepper. In the pot, add potatoes, bacon, and onions and top with the vinegar mixture. Seal the lid and cook for 6 minutes on High Pressure. Release pressure naturally for 10 minutes. Transfer to a serving plate. Enjoy!

Delicious Broccoli & Cauliflower Salad

Serving Size: 4 | **Total Time:** 10 minutes

1 lb cauliflower florets
1 lb broccoli, into florets
3 garlic cloves, crushed
¼ tbsp olive oil
1 tsp salt
1 tbsp dry rosemary

Cut the veggies into bite-sized pieces and place them in the pot. Add olive oil and 1 cup of water. Season with salt, garlic, and rosemary. Seal the lid. Cook on High Pressure for 3 minutes. When ready, do a quick release.

Greek-Style Pasta Salad

Serving Size: 6 | **Total Time:** 15 minutes

1 lb rotini pasta
2 plum tomatoes, halved
1 cucumber, sliced
1 red bell pepper, diced
¼ cup extra-virgin olive oil
2 tbsp white wine vinegar
1 cup feta, crumbled
2 tbsp fresh dill, chopped

Cover the rotini pasta with salted water in your Instant Pot and seal the lid. Select Manual and cook for 4 minutes on High. When ready, perform a quick pressure release and unlock the lid. Drain the pasta and set aside. Mix the extra-virgin olive oil, white wine vinegar, and salt in a large serving bowl. Add in the cooked pasta, tomatoes, cucumber, and bell pepper and toss to combine. Top with feta cheese and dill and serve.

BROTHS & SAUCES

Herbed Squash Sauce

Serving Size: 4 | **Total Time:** 30 minutes

2 cups butternut squash, peeled, cubed
3 beets, trimmed, peeled, cubed
3 carrots, peeled, cubed
1 cup red wine
1 tsp dried basil
1 tbsp dried parsley
1 tsp dried oregano, ground
½ tsp garlic powder
Salt and pepper to taste

Add squash, beets, and carrots to your Instant Pot. Pour in 2 cups of water and seal the lid. Press Manual and set the timer to 10 minutes n High. Do a quick pressure release. Carefully unlock the lid. Transfer to a food processor and pulse until smooth and creamy. Add wine, basil, parsley, oregano, garlic powder, salt, and pepper and blend for a minute. Return to the pot, press Sauté, and cook for 10 minutes, stirring occasionally. Serve.

Garlic Red Bell Pepper Sauce

Serving Size: 3 | **Total Time:** 15 minutes

3 red bell peppers, chopped
1 cup cherry tomatoes, diced
1 onion, chopped
1 tsp garlic powder
½ cup sour cream
2 cups vegetable broth
1 tbsp balsamic vinegar
1 tbsp cayenne pepper

Combine bell peppers, cherry tomatoes, onion, garlic powder, sour cream, broth, balsamic vinegar, and cayenne pepper in a mixing bowl. Add the mixture to the Instant Pot, seal the lid, and cook on High Pressure for 6 minutes. When ready, do a quick release. Carefully unlock the lid. Transfer to your food processor and purée until the mixture is smooth. Serve and enjoy!

Quick Zucchini Sauce with Greek Yogurt

Serving Size: 4 | **Total Time:** 10 minutes

1 zucchini, chopped
1 cup Greek yogurt
1 cup sour cream
1 tsp garlic powder
¼ cup shallots, minced
Salt and pepper to taste

In the pot, mix zucchini, sour cream, garlic, shallots, salt, and pepper and stir until combined. Seal the lid and cook on High Pressure for 3 minutes. Do a quick release. Remove the sauce to a bowl and stir in the yogurt. Serve.

Mediterranean Tomato Sauce

Serving Size: 4 | **Total Time:** 15 minutes

2 cups tomatoes, diced
½ cup tomato sauce
½ cup sun-dried tomatoes
1 medium onion, chopped
3 tbsp balsamic vinegar
3 garlic cloves, chopped
1 tsp dried oregano
1 tbsp olive oil
Salt and pepper to taste

Combine tomatoes, tomato sauce, sun-dried tomatoes, onion, balsamic vinegar, garlic, oregano, oil, salt, and pepper in a mixing bowl and give it a good stir. Transfer to the Instant Pot and seal the lid. Cook on High Pressure for 6 minutes. When done, remove to serving bowls and serve with pasta or rice.

Caprese Sauce with Goat Cheese

Serving Size: 4 | **Total Time:** 15 minutes

1 cup goat cheese, crumbled
1 cup tomatoes, diced
3 tbsp tomato paste
1 onion, finely chopped
3 tbsp apple cider vinegar
3 garlic cloves, chopped
¼ cup mozzarella cheese
2 cups vegetable broth
Salt and pepper to taste

Add goat cheese, tomatoes, tomato paste, onion, vinegar, garlic, mozzarella cheese, broth, salt, and pepper to your Instant Pot, seal the lid and cook on High Pressure for 6 minutes. When done, press Cancel and do a quick pressure release. Serve.

Homemade Honey Applesauce

Serving Size: 4 | **Total Time:** 25 minutes

4 apples, cored, chopped
1 tsp ground cinnamon
1 tsp honey

Add apples, cinnamon, ½ cup water, and honey. Seal the lid and cook on High Pressure for 4 minutes. Release Pressure naturally for 10 minutes. If you desire a chunky blend, stir vigorously. For smooth applesauce, puree the mixture in a blender. Allow to cool before transferring in containers for storage.

Spicy Green Sauce

Serving Size: 4 | **Total Time:** 10 minutes

4 oz green jalapeño peppers, chopped
1 green bell pepper, chopped
2 garlic cloves, crushed
½ cup white vinegar
1 tbsp apple cider vinegar
1 tsp salt

Add jalapeño peppers, bell pepper, garlic, white vinegar, apple vinegar, and salt to the Instant Pot. Pour in 4 tbsp water. Seal the lid and cook on High Pressure for 2 minutes. When done, release the steam naturally for about 5 minutes. Transfer to a blender, pulse until combined, and store in jars.

SOUPS

Corn Soup with Chicken & Egg

Serving Size: 2 | **Total Time:** 25 minutes
1 tbsp cilantro, chopped
1 egg
½ lb chicken breasts
1 leek, chopped
1 tbsp sliced shallots
¼ tsp nutmeg
2 cups water
¼ cup corn kernels
¼ cup diced carrots
Salt and pepper to taste

Slice the chicken breasts into small cubes and place them in your Instant Pot. Add in corn kernels, water, shallots, salt, nutmeg, and black pepper. Seal the lid, select Pressure Cook, and cook for 15 minutes on High.

When done, allow a natural release and unlock the lid. Mix in carrots and leek and bring to a boil on Sauté. Beat the egg in a bowl. Once the Soup boil, pour in the beaten egg and toss until well combined and done. Divide between bowls, sprinkle with cilantro, and serve.

Mustard Carrot Soup

Serving Size: 4 | **Total Time:** 25 minutes
1 green bell pepper, diced
¼ cup butter
1 lb quartered carrots
3 cups chicken stock
1 tsp paprika
1 tsp ground cumin
2 tsp minced garlic
2 tbsp Dijon mustard
Salt and pepper to taste

Pour 1 cup of water into your Instant Pot; fit in a trivet. Place the carrots on the trivet and seal the lid. Select Manual and cook for 1 minute on High. When done, perform a quick pressure release; unlock the lid. Remove the carrots and pat dry the pot with a paper towel.

Melt butter in your Instant Pot on Sauté. Place the chicken stock, paprika, bell pepper, cumin, garlic, mustard, salt, black pepper, and cooked carrots. Seal the lid, select Manual, and cook for 4 minutes on High pressure.

When done, allow a natural release for 10 minutes and unlock the lid. Using an immersion blender, blend the soup until smooth and creamy. Serve right away.

Easy Veggie Soup

Serving Size: 4 | **Total Time:** 35 minutes

1 cup okra, trimmed
1 Carrot, sliced
1 cup Broccoli florets
1 green Bell Pepper, sliced
1 red Bell Pepper, sliced
1 Onion, sliced
2 cups vegetable broth
1 tbsp Lemon juice
4 Garlic cloves, minced
Salt and pepper to taste
2 tbsp Olive oil

Warm olive oil in your Instant Pot on Sauté. Place the onion and garlic and cook for 1 minute. Add in carrot, okra, broccoli florets, green bell pepper, and red bell pepper and cook for 5-10 minutes.

Stir in vegetable broth, salt, and black pepper and seal the lid. Select Meat/Stew and cook for 15 minutes on High pressure. When done, perform a quick pressure release and unlock the lid. Sprinkle with lemon juice and divide between bowls before serving.

Cheesy & Creamy Broccoli Soup

Serving Size: 4 | **Total Time:** 25 minutes

1 ½ cups grated Cheddar Cheese + extra for topping
2 tbsp cilantro, chopped
1 lb chopped Broccoli
3 cups Heavy Cream
3 cups Chicken Broth
4 tbsp Butter
4 tbsp Almond flour
1 red onion, chopped
3 garlic cloves, minced
1 tsp Italian Seasoning
Salt and pepper to taste
4 oz Cream Cheese

Melt butter in your Instant Pot on Sauté. Place the almond flour and stir until it clumps up. Slowly pour in heavy cream and stir until it gets a sauce. Remove to a bowl. Put the onions, garlic, chicken broth, broccoli, Italian seasoning, and cream cheese in the pot and stir.

Seal the lid, select Soup, and cook for 15 minutes on High pressure. When done, perform a quick pressure release and unlock the lid. Mix in butter sauce and cheddar cheese until the cheese melts. Divide between bowls and top with cheddar cheese. Serve topped with cilantro.

Gingery Carrot Soup

Serving Size: 2 | **Total Time:** 30 minutes

½ tsp red pepper flakes
2 cups chicken broth
½ lb carrots, chopped
½ tbsp Sriracha sauce
1 cup canned coconut milk
1 tbsp cilantro, chopped
1 tbsp unsalted butter
½ tsp fresh ginger, minced
1 garlic clove, minced
1 small onion, chopped

Place the butter and onion in your Instant Pot and cook for 2-3 minutes until soft on Sauté. Add in ginger and garlic and cook for 1 minute. Stir in carrots and cook for 2 minutes. Mix in coconut milk, chicken broth, red pepper flakes, and Sriracha and seal the lid.

Select Manual and cook for 6 minutes on High. When done, allow a natural release for 10 minutes; unlock the lid. Using an immersion blender, pulse the soup until purée. Serve topped with cilantro. Enjoy!

Carrot & Cabbage Soup

Serving Size: 4 | **Total Time:** 25 minutes

1 cup canned white beans
14 oz can diced tomatoes
1 head cabbage, chopped
3 tbsp Apple cider vinegar
4 minced garlic cloves
4 cup chicken broth
1 chopped celery stalk
3 chopped carrots
1 tbsp lemon juice
1 chopped onion

Place the chopped tomatoes, cabbage, apple cider vinegar, garlic, chicken broth, celery, carrots, lemon juice, and onion in your Instant Pot. Seal the lid, select Manual, and cook for 15 minutes on High pressure. When done, perform a quick pressure release and unlock the lid. Mix in white beans and cook for 2 minutes on Sauté. Serve.

Scallion Chicken & Lentil Soup

Serving Size: 4 | **Total Time:** 45 minutes

4 garlic cloves, sliced
6 oz skinless chicken thighs
½ lb dried lentils
½ chopped onion
4 cups water
¼ tsp paprika
½ tsp garlic powder
1 diced tomato
2 tbsp chopped cilantro
¼ tsp oregano
½ tsp cumin
1 chopped scallion
¼ tsp salt

Place the chicken thighs, dried lentils, onion, water, paprika, garlic powder, sliced garlic, tomato, cilantro, oregano, cumin, scallion, and salt in your Instant Pot. Seal the lid, select Soup, and cook for 30 minutes. When done, allow a natural release for 10 minutes and unlock the lid. Using a fork, shred the chicken before serving.

Tomato Shrimp Soup

Serving Size: 4 | **Total Time:** 40 minutes

½ cup coconut Cream
2 Tomatoes, sliced
2 oz Shrimp
4 cups Chicken broth
¼ cup Apple Cider Vinegar
2 Garlic cloves, minced
Salt and pepper to taste
1 tbsp Olive oil

Warm olive oil in your Instant Pot on Sauté. Place the garlic and cook for 1 minute. Add in shrimp and cook for 10 minutes. Stir in salt, black pepper, chicken broth, tomatoes, and apple cider vinegar.

Seal the lid, select Manual, and cook for 10 minutes on High pressure. When done, allow a natural release for 10 minutes and unlock the lid. Divide between 4 bowls and top each with coconut cream. Serve warm.

Mustard Potato Soup with Crispy Bacon

Serving Size: 4 | **Total Time:** 30 minutes

2 Yukon gold potatoes, chopped
2 tbsp olive oil
2 garlic cloves, minced
1 leek, diced
1 tbsp onion powder
1 green bell pepper, diced
4 cups chicken stock
Salt and pepper to taste
1 tbsp Dijon mustard
4 dashes hot pepper sauce
4 oz bacon, chopped
2 cups shredded mozzarella
1 cup milk

Warm olive oil in your Instant Pot on Sauté and cook the bacon for 5 minutes until crispy; set aside. Place garlic and leek in the pot and sauté for 3 minutes. Add in onion powder, potatoes, bell pepper, stock, salt, and pepper. Seal the lid, select Manual, and cook for 15 minutes.

When done, perform a quick pressure release. Mix in Dijon mustard, hot sauce, mozzarella cheese, and milk until thoroughly heated. Top with bacon and serve.

Curried Pumpkin Soup

Serving Size: 4 | **Total Time:** 20 minutes

1 tsp chili powder
2 tbsp Pumpkin seeds
2 tbsp Olive oil
1 onion, chopped
1 Carrot, chopped
2 garlic cloves, minced
2 tsp Curry powder
4 cups vegetable broth

Warm olive oil in your Instant Pot on Sauté. Place the onion and garlic and cook for 3 minutes until tender. Add in vegetable broth, pumpkin seeds, chili powder, curry powder, and carrots. Seal the lid, select Manual, and cook for 10 minutes on High. When done, allow a natural release for 10 minutes. Serve.

Nutmeg Broccoli Soup with Cheddar

Serving Size: 4 | **Total Time:** 25 minutes

2 garlic cloves, minced
1 tbsp butter
½ lb broccoli florets
¼ tsp nutmeg
½ tsp garlic powder
1 cup vegetable broth
¼ cup grated cheddar
¼ cup chopped onion
¼ tsp paprika
Salt and pepper to taste

Melt butter in your Instant Pot on Sauté. Place the onion and garlic and cook until wilted and aromatic. Put in vegetable broth, broccoli, black pepper, paprika, salt, nutmeg, and garlic powder. Seal the lid, select Manual, and cook for 5 minutes on High pressure.

When done, allow a natural release for 10 minutes and unlock the lid. Using an immersion blender, pulse the soup until smooth. Divide between bowls and serve.

Kielbasa Sausage Soup

Serving Size: 4 | **Total Time:** 60 minutes

12 oz Kielbasa smoked sausage, sliced
2 tbsp olive oil
1 yellow onion, chopped
1 celery stalk, chopped
1 carrot, chopped
2 tbsp parsley, chopped
3 garlic cloves, pressed
1 ripe tomato, pureed
1 cup pinto beans, soaked
Salt and pepper to taste
6 oz baby kale

Warm the olive oil in your Instant Pot on Sauté. Add in onion, garlic, celery, and carrot and cook for 4 minutes. Stir in smoked sausage for another 2 minutes and pour in pinto beans, salt, pepper, and 4 cups of water. Seal the lid, select Manual, and cook for 30 minutes on High.

When over, allow a natural release for 10 minutes and unlock the lid. Stir in baby kale and tomato and let it sit covered for 5 minutes. Serve sprinkled with parsley.

Chorizo & Bean Soup

Serving Size: 6 | **Total Time:** 55 minutes

2 tbsp olive oil
¾ lb chorizo sausage, sliced
1 cup white beans, soaked
1 sweet pepper, sliced
14 oz can diced tomatoes
1 clove garlic, minced
1 onion, diced
½ tsp dried oregano
1 tsp chili powder
6 cups chicken broth

Warm the olive oil in your Instant Pot on Sauté. Add in onion, garlic, chorizo, sweet pepper, chili powder, and oregano and cook for 4-5 minutes. Stir in chicken broth, tomatoes, and white bean and seal the lid. Select Manual and cook for 30 minutes. Once ready, perform a quick pressure release and let sit for 10 minutes. Serve warm.

Beet & Potato Soup

Serving Size: 4 | **Total Time:** 45 minutes

2 tbsp olive oil
2 garlic cloves, minced
1 carrot, chopped
3 potatoes, chopped
¾ lb beets, peeled, chopped
4 cups vegetable broth
1 onion, chopped
Salt and pepper to taste
¼ cup basil leaves, chopped

Heat the olive oil in your Instant Pot on Sauté. Place the onion, carrot, and garlic paste and cook for 3 minutes. Stir in vegetable broth, beets, and potatoes and seal the lid. Select Manual and cook for 25 minutes.

Once ready, allow a natural release for 10 minutes, then perform a quick pressure release and unlock the lid. Blend the soup using an immersion blender and adjust the seasoning. Serve topped with basil.

Vegan Tomato Soup

Serving Size: 4 | **Total Time**: 20 minutes

2 tbsp olive oil
2 (14-oz) cans tomatoes
1 tsp caraway seeds
1 cup vegetable broth
½ tsp thyme
1 large onion, diced
2 garlic cloves, sliced
Salt and pepper to taste
¾ cup almond milk

Warm the olive oil in your Instant Pot on Sauté. Add in onion, and garlic and cook for 5-6 minutes until lightly golden. Stir in caraway seeds for 1 minute and pour in tomatoes, thyme, and vegetable broth.

Seal the lid, select Manual, and cook for 8 minutes on High. Once ready, perform a quick pressure release and unlock the lid. Stir in almond milk and adjust the seasonings. Purée the soup with an immersion blender.

Asian Tomato Soup

Serving Size: 8 | **Total Time**: 20 minutes

2 tbsp coconut oil
1 onion, diced
1 tbsp garlic-ginger puree
3 lb tomatoes, quartered
½ tsp ground cumin
1 tsp red pepper flakes
Pink salt to taste
3 ½ cups vegetable broth
1 cup coconut cream
2 tbsp cilantro, chopped

Heat the coconut oil in your Instant Pot on Sauté. Place the onion and garlic-ginger paste and cook for 3 minutes. Stir in tomatoes and cumin and Sauté for 3 more minutes.

Pour in the broth and salt and seal the lid. Select Manual and cook for 6 minutes. When done, perform a quick pressure release. Mix in coconut cream. Puree the soup with a stick blender until smooth. Serve topped with red pepper flakes and cilantro.

Tangy Pumpkin Soup

Serving Size: 4 | **Total Time:** 30 minutes

2 tbsp sesame oil
1 yellow onion, chopped
2 garlic cloves, minced
½ tbsp ginger, grated
1 lb pumpkin, cubed
Salt to taste
1 tbsp curry powder
1 tsp cayenne pepper
½ cup coconut milk
2 tbsp cilantro, chopped

Warm the sesame oil in your Instant Pot on Sauté. Add in onion and cook for 5 minutes. Stir in garlic and ginger and Sauté for 1 more minute. Stir in pumpkin, cayenne pepper, salt, and curry powder and 4 cups of water and seal the lid. Select Manual and cook for 20 minutes. Once ready, perform a quick pressure release and unlock the lid. Blend the soup using a stick blender and mix in coconut milk. Garnish with cilantro and serve.

Chicken Soup with Vegetables

Serving Size: 4 | **Total Time:** 35 minutes

½ lb chicken breasts, cubed
1 beet, chopped
1 carrot, diced
½ celery, diced
1 onion, chopped
1 cup mushrooms, sliced
5 cups chicken stock
2 garlic cloves, chopped
1 tsp thyme
1 tsp rosemary
2 bay leaves
2 tbsp olive oil
Salt and pepper to taste

Warm olive oil in your Instant Pot on Sauté. Place the carrots, beet, and onion and cook for 2-3 minutes. Add in garlic, celery, and mushrooms and cook for 3 minutes. Put in chicken breasts, chicken stock, thyme, rosemary, bay leaves, salt, and black pepper. Seal the lid, select Soup, and cook on Low pressure for 20 minutes. When done, perform a quick pressure release. Serve warm.

Celery & Oxtail Soup

Serving Size: 4 | **Total Time:** 30 minutes

4 cups vegetable broth
2 tbsp chopped' carrots
1 lb oxtails
1 tbsp chopped' celeries
¼ tsp nutmeg
Salt and pepper to taste

Place the oxtails, nutmeg, salt, and black pepper in your Instant Pot. Pour in vegetable broth and seal the lid. Select Pressure Cook and cook for 20 minutes on High.

When done, perform a quick pressure release and unlock the lid. Stir in chopped carrots and celeries and cook for 3 minutes until the carrots are tender on Sauté. Divide between bowls and serve.

Creamy Mushroom Soup with Chicken

Serving Size: 2 | **Total Time:** 20 minutes

1 celery stalk, chopped
¼ cup diced mushrooms
½ lb chicken breasts
¼ cup heavy cream
½ cup water
2 tbsp diced carrots
1 tsp minced' garlic
Salt and pepper to taste

Slice the chicken breast into small cubes and remove them to your Instant Pot. Add in celery, minced garlic, salt, black pepper, and water. Seal the lid, select Pressure Cook, and cook for 10 minutes on High pressure.

When done, perform a quick pressure release and unlock the lid. Stir in heavy cream, mushrooms, and carrots. Seal the lid, select Manual, and cook for 3 minutes on High pressure. When done, perform a quick pressure release and unlock the lid. Divide between bowls and serve.

Cheesy Cauliflower Soup

Serving Size: 4 | **Total Time:** 20 minutes

2 tbsp olive oil
1 carrot, chopped
¼ cup cream cheese
1 ½ cups cauliflower florets
1 cup vegetable broth
2 tsp minced garlic
¼ cup chopped onion
Salt and pepper to taste

Warm the olive oil in your Instant Pot on Sauté. Place the cauliflower florets, carrot, minced garlic, chopped onion, salt, and pepper and cook for 5 minutes until tender. pour in the vegetable broth. Seal the lid, select Manual, and cook for 6 minutes on High pressure.

When done, perform a quick pressure release and unlock the lid. Mix in cream cheese until well combined. Blend the soup until smooth with an immersion blender. Divide between bowls and serve.

Spicy Ground Beef Soup

Serving Size: 4 | **Total Time:** 30 minutes

2 tbsp butter
3 oz cream cheese
7-oz ground beef
4 cups beef broth
2 garlic cloves, minced
1 tsp chili powder
1 tsp ground cumin
½ cup heavy cream
Salt and pepper to taste

Melt butter in your Instant Pot on Sauté. Place the ground beef and cook for 5-7 minutes and strain excess fat. Add in cream cheese, garlic, chili powder, ground cumin, heavy cream, salt, black pepper, and beef broth.

Seal the lid, select Pressure Cook, and cook for 5 minutes on High pressure. When done, allow a natural release for 10 minutes and unlock the lid. Serve warm.

Hot Spinach Soup

Serving Size: 4 | **Total Time:** 50 minutes

1 onion, chopped
2 Garlic cloves, minced
1 cup baby Spinach
2 cups Vegetable broth
½ cup Almond Milk
½ tbsp Chili flakes
¼ cup sour cream
2 tbsp Olive oil

Place the garlic, onion, spinach, vegetable broth, almond milk, chili flakes, and olive oil in your Instant Pot. Seal the lid, select Manual, and cook for 25 minutes on High.

When done, allow a natural release for 10 minutes and unlock the lid. Using an immersion blender, blend until creamy and put it back to the pot and cook for 6 minutes on Sauté. Serve topped with sour cream.

Asian-Style Chicken Soup

Serving Size: 4 | **Total Time:** 35 minutes

1 tsp soy sauce
4 cups chicken broth
½ lb chicken breasts, cubed
1 tsp cinnamon
1 tsp cilantro, chopped
1 tbsp olive oil
1 tbsp fish sauce
1 tsp ginger
1 tbsp sugar
1 chopped onion
2 tsp minced garlic
Salt and pepper to taste

Place the olive oil, garlic, and onion in your Instant Pot and cook for 2-3 minutes until soft on Sauté. Stir in chopped chicken, ginger, cilantro, sugar, cinnamon, fish sauce, soy sauce, salt, pepper, and chicken broth. Seal the lid, select Manual, and cook for 15 minutes on High. When done, allow a natural release for 10 minutes. Serve.

Egg & Chicken Soup

Serving Size: 4 | **Total Time:** 35 minutes

1 carrot, chopped
2 Garlic cloves, minced
¼ lb chicken breasts, cubed
1 onion, chopped
2 Eggs, whisked
2 cups Chicken broth
2 cups Water
3 tbsp Almond flour
Salt and pepper to taste
2 tbsp Olive oil

Warm olive oil in your Instant Pot on Sauté. Place the carrot, garlic, and onion and cook for 1 minute. Add in chicken pieces and cook for 10 minutes. Put in salt, black pepper, and chicken broth and simmer for 15 minutes.

Meanwhile, combine water and almond flour in a bowl and pour it slowly into the pot and cook for 2 minutes. Add in eggs and cook for 2 more minutes. Divide between bowls and serve.

Cheesy Chicken Soup

Serving Size: 4 | **Total Time:** 30 minutes

2 garlic cloves, minced
1 green bell pepper, sliced
1 red bell pepper, sliced
½ cup chicken breast strips
1 tbsp canola oil
1 tsp dried oregano
1 onion, sliced
4 oz Provolone cheese, grated
4 cups Chicken broth
Salt and pepper to taste

Place the canola oil and chicken fillets in your Instant Pot and cook on Sauté. Mix in oregano, salt, black pepper, red bell pepper, green bell pepper, garlic, and onion and cook for 10 minutes. Pour in chicken broth and seal the lid. Select Manual and cook for 4 minutes on High pressure. When done, allow a natural release for 10 minutes and unlock the lid. Serve topped with cheese.

Brussel Sprout & Pork Soup

Serving Size: 4 | **Total Time:** 40 minutes

½ lb Brussels sprouts, shredded
1 cup carrot, shredded
½ tsp ground ginger
1 small onion, chopped
½ lb ground pork
4 cups chicken broth
1 tbsp soy sauce
2 tbsp olive oil
Salt and pepper to taste

Place the olive oil and ground pork in your Instant Pot and cook for 4-5 minutes until browned on Sauté. Stir in carrot, Brussels sprouts, ginger, onion, chicken broth, soy sauce, salt, and black pepper. Seal the lid, select Manual, and cook for 25 minutes on High pressure. When done, perform a quick pressure release. Serve and enjoy!

Tamarind Beef Soup

Serving Size: 2 | **Total Time:** 40 minutes

1 carrot, sliced
¼ cup green tomatoes
1 lb beef tenderloin
1 cup water
2 tsp tamarind
1 tsp soy sauce
2 tsp sliced garlic
2 tsp sliced shallots
2 tsp red chili flakes
½ tsp salt

Slice the beef tenderloin into medium pieces and place them in your Instant Pot. Add in garlic, carrot, shallots, red chili flakes, salt, green tomatoes, tamarind, soy sauce, and water. Seal the lid, select Manual, and cook for 22 minutes on High. When done, allow a natural release for 10 minutes and unlock the lid. Serve warm.

Cashew & Tomato Soup

Serving Size: 4 | **Total Time:** 15 minutes

½ ground cumin
15 oz tomato puree
15 oz diced tomatoes
4 tbsp cashew
2 cups vegetable stock
½ tbsp dried basil
1 ½ tbsp quick oats
2 minced garlic cloves
Salt and pepper to taste

Place the tomato puree, diced tomatoes, cashew, vegetable stock, dried basil, oats, cumin, and garlic in your Instant Pot. Seal the lid, select Manual, and cook for 4 minutes on High pressure. When done, allow a natural release. Using an immersion blender, pulse the soup until smooth. Sprinkle with salt and pepper before serving.

Pecorino Mushroom Soup

Serving Size: 4 | **Total Time:** 30 minutes

2 cups Pecorino, grated
3 cups Mushrooms, chopped
2 tbsp Butter
1 onion, chopped
2 Garlic cloves, minced
2 cups Thyme, chopped
2 tbsp Almond flour
3 cups Chicken stock

Place the butter and onion in your Instant Pot and cook for 2 minutes on Sauté. Mix in mushrooms, garlic cloves, thyme, chicken stock, and almond flour. Seal the lid, select Manual, and cook for 10 minutes on High. When done, allow a natural release for 10 minutes. Serve garnished with grated Pecorino cheese.

Creamy Chicken & Zucchini Soup

Serving Size: 4 | **Total Time**: 25 minutes

1 lb Zucchini, chopped
1 lb Chicken breasts, cubed
2 tbsp Butter
1 onion, chopped
2 Garlic cloves, minced
4 cups Chicken broth
2 tbsp Nutmeg powder
½ cup Half and Half

Melt butter in your Instant Pot on Sauté. Mix the zucchini, chicken broth, garlic, onion, nutmeg powder, chicken cubes, and half and half. Seal the lid, select Manual, and cook for 10 minutes on High pressure. When done, allow a natural release for 10 minutes and unlock the lid. Serve right away.

Quick Chicken Soup

Serving Size: 4 | **Total Time**: 25 minutes

½ cup mushrooms, chopped
½ lb Chicken Breasts
2 tbsp Olive oil
1 large Carrot, chopped
1 Celery Stalk, chopped
1 onion, chopped
2 garlic cloves, minced
1 Green Chili Pepper, sliced
Salt and pepper to taste
2 cups Chicken Broth

Warm olive oil in your Instant Pot on Sauté. Place the carrot, celery, onion, garlic, salt, pepper, and green chili pepper and cook for 3 minutes. Mix in broth, chicken breasts, mushrooms, and 2 cups of water. Seal the lid, select Soup, and cook for 10 minutes on High. Do a quick pressure release. Remove the chicken, shred it, and back it to the pot. Cook for 3 minutes on Sauté and serve.

Chicken & Noodle Soup

Serving Size: 2 | **Total Time**: 35 minutes

8 oz egg noodles
2 Carrots, sliced
1 tbsp Olive Oil
1 small onion, chopped
2 Celery Ribs, diced
1 Banana Pepper, minced
1 garlic clove, minced
1 small Bay Leaf
2 Chicken Breasts
3 cups Chicken Broth

Warm olive oil in your Instant Pot on Sauté. Place the onion, celery, carrots, garlic, and banana pepper and cook for 4 minutes. Add in bay leaf, chicken, and broth. Seal the lid, select Manual, and cook for 15 minutes on High. When done, perform a quick pressure release. Transfer the chicken onto a cutting board and shred it. Put the chicken back in the pot with the egg noodles and cook for 7-8 minutes on Sauté. Serve.

Simple Onion Cheese Soup

Serving Size: 4 | **Total Time**: 10 minutes

1 onion, chopped
2 tbsp all-purpose flour
4 cups vegetable broth
2 cups Monterey Jack, grated
2 cups milk
2 tbsp butter

Melt butter on Sauté and cook the onion and flour for 2 minutes. Gradually stir in the broth and milk. Seal the lid. Cook on High Pressure for 5 minutes. Do a quick pressure release. Stir in cheese until melted. Serve.

STEWS

Rabbit & Veggie Stew

Serving Size: 6 | **Total Time:** 55 minutes

1 rabbit, cut into chunks
4 tbsp olive oil
1 cup dry red wine
1 onion, chopped
2 garlic cloves, minced
1 carrot, chopped
1 cup mushrooms, sliced
1 zucchini, chopped
2 celery stalks, chopped
2 tomatoes, diced
1 tbsp tomato paste
1 bunch rosemary sprigs
1 bay leaf
3 cups chicken broth
Salt and pepper to taste
2 tbsp parsley, chopped

Sprinkle rabbit with salt and pepper. Warm the olive oil in your Instant Pot on Sauté. Place in rabbit chunks and cook for 5 minutes on all sides; reserve. Stir onion, garlic, carrot, celery, mushrooms, and zucchini for 4-5 minutes until tender. Add in red wine tomatoes, tomato paste, bay leaf, and rosemary and cook for 5 minutes.

Mix in chicken broth, return the rabbit, and seal the lid. Select Manual and cook for 15 minutes on High pressure. Once done, allow a natural release for 10 minutes, then perform a quick pressure release, and unlock the lid. Adjust season to taste and discard rosemary sprigs and bay leaf. Serve topped with parsley.

Thyme Chicken Pot with Cheese

Serving Size: 4 | **Total Time**: 30 minutes
1 carrot, chopped
1 lb Chicken breasts, cubed
1 Onion, chopped
3 Garlic cloves, minced
2 oz Parmesan cheese, grated
Salt and pepper to taste
¼ tbsp Thyme
2 tbsp Butter

Melt butter in your Instant Pot on Sauté. Add in onion and garlic and sauté for 2-3 minutes until translucent. Put in chicken breast and cook until golden brown, 6-8 minutes. Stir in carrot, salt, black pepper, thyme, and 3 cups of water. Seal the lid, select Manual, and cook for 20 minutes on High pressure. When done, perform a quick pressure release. Serve sprinkled with Parmesan.

Coconut & Cauliflower Curry

Serving Size: 4 | **Total Time**: 25 minutes
2 tbsp butter
1 onion, chopped
3 cups chicken broth
1 cup coconut milk
2 tbsp red curry paste
½ tsp cardamom
½ tsp cumin
1 head cauliflower, chopped
1 tbsp cilantro, chopped

Melt the butter in your Instant Pot on Sauté. Place the onion and cook for 4-5 minutes. Add in chicken broth, cauliflower, coconut milk, curry paste, cardamon, and cumin and seal the lid. Select Manual and cook for 10 minutes on High pressure. When ready, perform a quick pressure release and unlock the lid. Blend the soup using an immersion blender. Serve topped cilantro.

Pancetta & Cheese Chicken Thighs

Serving Size: 4 | **Total Time:** 30 minutes
4 Bacon Slices, cooked and crumbled
1 cup Chicken Broth
4 Chicken Thighs
8 oz Cream Cheese
½ cup shredded Cheddar
¼ tsp Garlic Powder
¼ tsp Italian Seasoning
Salt and pepper to taste
2 tbsp Arrowroot

Combine the chicken broth, cream cheese, garlic powder, Italian seasoning, salt, and black pepper in your Instant Pot. Add in chicken thighs and seal the lid. Select Manual and cook for 18 minutes on High pressure. When done, perform a quick pressure release and unlock the lid. Transfer the chicken to a plate. Add the arrowroot to the pot and cook for 2 minutes until the sauce thickens on Sauté. Mix in pancetta and chicken and serve right away.

Habanero Chicken Stew

Serving Size: 4 | **Total Time:** 25 minutes
1 habanero pepper, diced
2 tbsp Butter
½ cup Hot Sauce
1 ½ cups Chicken Broth
½ Onion, diced
2 Garlic Cloves, minced
1 cup Heavy Cream
2 cups shredded Cheddar
2 Chicken Breasts
1 Celery Stalk, diced
½ cup chopped Cauliflower
Salt and pepper to taste

Place the butter, hot sauce, chicken broth, onion, garlic, habanero pepper, chicken breasts, celery, cauliflower, salt, and pepper in your Instant Pot. Seal the lid, select Manual, and cook for 15 minutes on High. When done, perform a quick pressure release and unlock the lid. Mix in heavy cream and cheddar cheese. Serve.

Chinese-Style Chicken Stew with Broccoli

Serving Size: 4 | **Total Time:** 20 minutes
1 tsp Chinese Five-Spice seasoning
1 cup Coconut Aminos
4 Chicken Breasts
1 cup Chicken Broth
3 tbsp Olive oil
½ tsp Fish Sauce
1 inch Ginger, grated
1 garlic clove, minced
Salt and pepper to taste
4 cups Broccoli Florets
1 tbsp Sesame seeds
2 tbsp Arrowroot Flour

Place the chicken breasts, chicken broth, olive oil, garlic, ginger, coconut aminos, Chinese five-spice seasoning, black pepper, and salt in your Instant Pot. Seal the lid, select Manual, and cook for 8 minutes on High pressure.

When done, perform a quick pressure release. Whisk the arrowroot with 2 tbsp water in a bowl and pour it into the pot. Add in broccoli and cook for 5 minutes on Sauté. Stir in fish sauce. Serve garnished with sesame seeds.

Hot Beef Chili

Serving Size: 4 | **Total Time:** 35 minutes
1 lb ground beef
2 tbsp olive oil
1 red bell pepper, chopped
1 yellow bell pepper, diced
1 onion, chopped
2 cups tomatoes, chopped
2 carrots, chopped
1 tsp chili powder
2 tbsp Worcestershire sauce
2 tsp paprika
2 tbsp parsley, chopped
Salt and pepper to taste

Select Sauté and add the olive oil and ground beef. Cook the beef until it browns while stirring occasionally for about 8 minutes. Top it with the onion, bell peppers, tomatoes, carrots, chili powder, Worcestershire sauce, paprika, salt, and pepper. Stir the ingredients well. Seal the lid, and select Soup/Broth on High Pressure and cook for 20 minutes. Once the timer has ended, do a quick pressure release. Sprinkle with parsley and serve.

Delicious Thai Vegetable Stew

Serving Size: 4 | **Total Time:** 20 minutes

1 tbsp coconut oil
1 cup onion, chopped
1 tbsp fresh ginger, minced
2 garlic cloves, minced
3 carrots, chopped
1 red bell pepper, chopped
1 orange bell pepper, diced
1 (14-oz) can coconut milk
1 cup bok choy, chopped
½ cup water
2 tbsp red curry paste
Salt and pepper to taste

Melt coconut oil on Sauté. Add in onion, garlic, and ginger and cook for 3 minutes until soft. Mix in orange bell pepper, red bell pepper and carrots and cook for 3 minutes until the peppers become soft and tender.

Add curry paste, bok choy, coconut milk, and water and stir well to obtain a consistent color of the sauce. Seal lid. Cook for 1 minute on High Pressure. Release the pressure quickly. Adjust the seasoning and serve hot.

Garbanzo Stew with Onions & Tomatoes

Serving Size: 5 | **Total Time:** 35 minutes

1 lb chickpeas, soaked
3 purple onions, chopped
2 tomatoes, chopped
2 oz fresh parsley, chopped
3 cups vegetable broth
1 tbsp paprika
2 tbsp olive oil

Warm olive oil on Sauté and stir-fry the onions for 3 minutes. Add chickpeas, tomatoes, broth, parsley, and paprika. Seal the lid and cook on the Meat/Stew for 30 minutes on High. Do a quick release. Serve warm.

VEGAN & VEGETARIAN

Vegan Sloppy Joe's

Serving Size: 6 | **Total Time:** 40 minutes

3 tbsp olive oil
1 chopped onion
1 red bell pepper, diced
3 cups vegetable broth
1 cup green lentils
14 oz can diced tomatoes
1 tsp chili powder
1 tbsp mustard powder
1 tbsp brown sugar
Salt and pepper to taste
6 hamburger buns
3 dill pickles, sliced

Warm the olive oil in your Instant Pot. Place in onion and bell pepper and cook for 5 minutes. Stir in vegetable broth, lentils, tomatoes, mustard powder, chili powder, brown sugar, salt, and pepper. Seal the lid, select Manual, and cook for 15 minutes on High pressure. Once over, allow a natural release for 10 minutes and unlock the lid. To assemble, toast each bun and top with lentil mixture and a dill slice. Serve right away.

Sweet Polenta with Pistachios

Serving Size: 4 | **Total Time:** 20 minutes

½ cup honey
5 cups water
1 cup polenta
½ cup heavy cream
¼ tsp salt
¼ cup pistachios, toasted

Set your Instant Pot to Sauté. Place honey and water and bring to a boil, stirring often. Stir in polenta. Seal the lid, select Manual, and cook for 12 minutes on High.

When ready, perform a quick pressure release and unlock the lid. Mix in heavy cream and let sit for 1 minute. Sprinkle with salt to taste. Top with pistachios and serve.

Almond & Cherry Millet

Serving Size: 4 | **Total Time:** 25 minutes

½ cup chopped dried cherries
1 cup millet
½ cup almond milk
2 tbsp coconut oil
2 tbsp shaved almonds

Place millet, milk, 2 cups of water, cherries, and coconut oil in your Instant Pot. Seal the lid; select Manual, and cook for 10 minutes on High. Once done, allow a natural release for 10 minutes. Top with almonds and serve.

Basil Parmesan Sauce

Serving Size: 4 | **Total Time:** 10 minutes

1 cup fresh basil, torn
1 cup cream cheese
2 tbsp Parmesan, shredded
1 tbsp olive oil
Salt and pepper to taste
2 cups vegetable broth

In the Instant Pot, stir basil, cream cheese, Parmesan, oil, salt, pepper, and broth. Seal the lid and cook on High Pressure for 5 minutes. Do a quick pressure release and unlock the lid. Serve immediately.

Coconut Milk Millet Pudding

Serving Size: 4 | **Total Time:** 25 minutes

1 cup millet
1 cup coconut milk
4 dried prunes, chopped
Maple syrup for serving

Place the millet, milk, and prunes in your Instant Pot. Stir in 1 cup water. Seal the lid, select Manual, and cook for 10 minutes on High pressure. When ready, allow a natural release for 10 minutes. Drizzle with maple syrup.

Blueberry & Quinoa Porridge

Serving Size: 4 | **Total Time:** 20 minutes

½ cup quinoa
1 ½ cups milk
2 tbsp honey
½ tsp vanilla extract
3 tbsp blueberries

Place the quinoa, vanilla extract, milk, and ½ cup of water in your Instant Pot and stir. Seal the lid, select Manual, and cook for 1 minute on High pressure. Once ready, allow a natural release for 10 minutes and unlock the lid. Top with honey and blueberries and serve.

Carrot & Sweet Potato Thick Soup

Serving Size: 4 | **Total Time:** 40 minutes

4 sweet potatoes, cut into bite-sized pieces
2 carrots, chopped
1 onion, chopped
6 tbsp olive oil
2 tbsp tomato sauce
1 tbsp celery, chopped
1 tbsp parsley, chopped
Salt and pepper to taste

Heat olive oil on Sauté. Add onion, carrots, celery, and potatoes. Stir-fry for 2 minutes. Stir in 4 cups of water and tomato sauce. Seal the lid and cook for 25 minutes on High Pressure. Do a quick release. Open the pot and add celery, parsley, salt, and pepper. Seal again, and cook for 5 minutes on High. Do a quick release.

Coconut Millet Porridge

Serving Size: 2 | **Total Time:** 25 minutes

½ cup millet
½ cup coconut milk
2 tbsp coconut flakes
1 tbsp honey

Place millet, milk, and 1/2 cup of water in your Instant Pot. Seal the lid, select Manual, and cook for 10 minutes on High pressure. When over, allow a natural release for 10 minutes and unlock the lid. Drizzle with honey, top with coconut flakes, and serve.

Cheddar Cheese Sauce with Broccoli

Serving Size: 4 | **Total Time:** 15 minutes

1 cup broccoli, chopped
1 cup cream cheese
1 cup cheddar, shredded
3 cups chicken broth
Salt and pepper to taste
2 tsp dried rosemary

Mix broccoli, cream cheese, cheddar, broth, salt, pepper, and rosemary in a large bowl. Pour the mixture into the Instant Pot. Seal the lid and cook on High Pressure for 8 minutes. Do a quick release. Store for up to 5 days.

Hot Tofu Meatballs

Serving Size: 4 | **Total Time:** 35 minutes

1 lb tofu, crumbled
2 tbsp butter, melted
¼ cup almond meal
1 garlic clove, minced
2 tbsp olive oil
3 tbsp hot sauce
2 tbsp chopped scallions
Salt to taste

Mix the almond meal, tofu, garlic, salt, and scallions in a bowl. Make meatballs out of the mixture. Warm olive oil in your Instant Pot on Sauté. Place the meatballs and cook for 10 minutes until browned.

In the meantime, microwave the butter and hot sauce in a bowl. Combine and set aside. Place the meatballs in the pot and top with hot sauce and 1 cup of water. Seal the lid, select Manual, and cook for 15 minutes on High pressure. When done, perform a quick pressure release and unlock the lid. Serve immediately.

DESSERTS & DRINKS

Amazing Fruity Cheesecake

Serving Size: 6 | **Total Time:** 35 minutes

1 ½ cups graham cracker crust
1 cup raspberries
3 cups cream cheese
1 tbsp fresh orange juice
3 eggs
½ stick butter, melted
¾ cup sugar
1 tsp vanilla paste
1 tsp orange zest

Insert the tray into the pressure cooker, and add 1 cup of water. Grease a springform. Mix in graham cracker crust with sugar and butter in a bowl. Press the mixture to form a crust at the bottom. Blend the raspberries and cream cheese with an electric mixer. Crack in the eggs and keep mixing until well combined. Mix in orange juice, vanilla paste, and orange zest. Pour this mixture into the pan, and cover the pan with aluminum foil. Lay the springform on the tray. Select Pressure Cook and cook for 20 minutes on High. Once the cooking is complete, do a quick pressure release. Refrigerate the cheesecake.

Chocolate Quinoa Bowl

Serving Size: 4 | **Total Time:** 15 minutes

12 squares dark chocolate, shaved
2 tbsp cocoa powder
1 cup quinoa
2 tbsp maple syrup
½ tsp vanilla
A pinch of salt
1 tbsp sliced almonds

Put the quinoa, cocoa powder, maple syrup, vanilla, 2 ¼ cups water, and salt in your Instant Pot. Seal the lid, select Manual, and cook for a minute on High pressure. When ready, allow a natural release for 10 minutes and unlock the lid. Using a fork, fluff the quinoa. Top with almonds and dark chocolate and serve.

Simple Apple Cider with Orange Juice

Serving Size: 6 | **Total Time**: 20 minutes

6 green apples, chopped
¼ cup orange juice
2 cinnamon sticks

In a blender, add orange juice, apples, and 3 cups water and blend until smooth; use a fine-mesh strainer to strain and press using a spoon. Get rid of the pulp. In the pot, mix the apple puree and cinnamon sticks. Seal the lid and cook for 10 minutes on High Pressure. Release the Pressure naturally. Strain again and do away with the solids.

Spiced & Warming Mulled Wine

Serving Size: 6 | **Total Time**: 20 minutes

3 cups red wine
2 tangerines, sliced
¼ cup honey
6 whole cloves
6 whole black peppercorns
2 cardamom pods
8 cinnamon sticks
1 tsp fresh ginger, grated
1 tsp ground cinnamon

Add red wine, honey, cardamom, 2 cinnamon sticks, cloves, tangerine slices, ginger, and peppercorns. Seal the lid and cook for 5 minutes on High Pressure. Release pressure naturally for 10 minutes. Using a fine mesh strainer, strain the wine. Discard spices. Divide the warm wine into glasses. Garnish with cinnamon sticks to serve.

Walnut & Dark Chocolate Brownies

Serving Size: 6 | **Total Time:** 30 minutes

2 eggs
1/3 cup granulated sugar
¼ cup olive oil
1/3 cup flour
1/3 cup cocoa powder
1/3 cup dark chocolate chips
1/3 cup chopped walnuts
1 tbsp milk
½ tsp baking powder
1 tbsp vanilla extract

Add 1 cup of water and set a steamer rack into the cooker. Line a parchment paper on the steamer basket. In a bowl, beat eggs and sugar to mix until smooth. Stir in oil, cocoa, milk, baking powder, chocolate chips, flour, walnuts, vanilla, and sea salt. Transfer the batter to the prepared steamer basket. Arrange into an even layer. Seal the lid, press Cake, and cook for 20 minutes on High. Release the pressure quickly. Let cool before cutting into squares. Use powdered sugar to dust and serve.

Quick Coconut Treat with Pears

Serving Size: 2 | **Total Time:** 15 minutes

¼ cup flour
1 cup coconut milk
2 pears, peeled and diced
¼ cup shredded coconut

Combine flour, milk, pears, and shredded coconut in your Pressure cooker. Seal the lid, select Pressure Cook and set the timer to 5 minutes at High pressure. When ready, do a quick pressure release. Divide the mixture between two bowls. Serve.

Homemade Walnut Layer Cake

Serving Size: 6 | **Total Time:** 25 minutes

½ cup vanilla pudding powder
3 standard cake crusts
¼ cup granulated sugar
4 cups milk
10.5 oz chocolate chips
¼ cup walnuts, minced

Combine vanilla powder, sugar, and milk in the inner pot. Cook until the pudding thickens, stirring constantly on Sauté. Remove from the steel pot. Place one crust into a springform pan. Pour half of the pudding and sprinkle with minced walnuts and chocolate chips. Cover with another crust and repeat the process. Finish with the final crust and wrap in foil.

Insert the trivet, pour in 1 cup of water, and place springform pan on top. Seal the lid and cook for 10 minutes on High Pressure. Do a quick release. Refrigerate.

Creme Caramel with Whipped Cream

Serving Size: 4 | **Total Time:** 30 minutes + cooling time

½ cup granulated sugar
4 tbsp caramel syrup
3 eggs
½ tsp vanilla extract
½ tbsp milk
5 oz whipping cream

Combine milk, whipping cream, and vanilla extract in your Instant Pot. Press Sauté, and cook for 5 minutes, or until small bubbles form. Set aside. Using an electric mixer, whisk the eggs and sugar. Gradually add the cream mixture and whisk until well combined. Divide the caramel syrup between 4 ramekins. Fill with egg mixture and place them on the trivet. Pour in 1 cup water. Seal the lid and cook for 15 minutes on High Pressure. Do a quick release. Remove the ramekins and cool.

Plum & Almond Dessert

Serving Size: 6 | **Total Time:** 1 hour 50 minutes

6 lb sweet ripe plums, pits removed and halved
2 cups white sugar
1 cup almond flakes

Drizzle the plums with sugar. Toss to coat. Let it stand for about 1 hour to allow plums to soak up the sugar. Transfer the plum mixture to the Instant Pot and pour 1 cup of water. Seal the lid and cook on High Pressure for 30 minutes. Allow the Pressure to release naturally for 10 minutes. Serve topped with almond flakes.

APPENDIX : RECIPES INDEX

A

Almond & Cherry Millet 105
Amazing Fruity Cheesecake 108
Apricot Steel Cut Oats 72
Arugula Salad with Sweet Potatoes & Eggs 77
Asian Tomato Soup 89
Asian-Style Chicken Soup 93
Asian-Style Lamb Curry 50
Asparagus & Mushrooms with Bacon 9
Asparagus Wrapped in Parma Ham 41
Authentic German Salad with Bacon 77
Awesome Pork & Celery Soup 37

B

Balsamic Lamb 54
Basil Clams with Garlic & White Wine 62
Basil Parmesan Sauce 105
Beer-Steamed Mussels 61
Beet & Potato Soup 88
Black Squid Ink Tagliatelle 58
Blueberry & Quinoa Porridge 106
Brussel Sprout & Pork Soup 95
Buckwheat Pancake with Yogurt & Berries 8
Buffalo Chicken with Blue Cheese Sauce 11
Buffalo Turkey Chili 31
Butter & Wine Lobster Tails 56

C

Cajun Orange Pork Shoulder 38
Caprese Sauce with Goat Cheese 81
Caribbean Turkey Wings 29
Carrot & Cabbage Soup 84
Carrot & Sweet Potato Thick Soup 106
Cashew & Tomato Soup 96
Celery & Oxtail Soup 91
Cheddar Cheese Sauce with Broccoli 107
Cheesy & Creamy Broccoli Soup 83
Cheesy Cauliflower Soup 92
Cheesy Chicken Soup 94
Cheesy Polenta with Sundried Tomatoes 74
Cheesy Shrimp Scampi 55
Chicken & Bacon Cacciatore 18
Chicken & Noodle Soup 98
Chicken Gumbo 13
Chicken in Creamy Mushroom Sauce 17
Chicken Sandwiches with Barbecue Sauce 7
Chicken Soup with Vegetables 90
Chicken with Chili & Lime 15
Chicken with Port Wine Sauce 20
Chili Squid 60
Chinese Shrimp with Green Beans 55
Chinese-Style Chicken Stew with Broccoli 102
Chocolate Quinoa Bowl 108
Chorizo & Bean Soup 88
Clam & Corn Chowder 63
Coconut & Cauliflower Curry 100
Coconut Cherry Steel Cut Oats 73
Coconut Milk Millet Pudding 105
Coconut Millet Porridge 106
Coconut Rice Breakfast 66
Corn Soup with Chicken & Egg 82
Crab Pilaf with Broccoli & Asparagus 58
Cranberry Turkey with Hazelnuts 25
Creamy Chicken & Zucchini Soup 97
Creamy Mushroom Soup with Chicken 91
Creme Caramel with Whipped Cream 111
Creole Chicken with Rice 16
Cuban Mojo Chicken Tortillas 16
Cumin Chicken with Capers 19
Curried Pumpkin Soup 86
Curried Tofu with Vegetables 9

D

Delicious Broccoli & Cauliflower Salad 78

Delicious Pork & Vegetables Soup 37
Delicious Thai Vegetable Stew 103
Delicious Turkey Burgers 22
Duck Breasts with Honey-Mustard Glaze 36

E

Easy Lamb & Spinach Soup 42
Easy Veggie Soup 83
Egg & Chicken Soup 94

F

Fennel Chicken with Tomato Sauce 13
Fennel Lamb Ribs 51
Feta Cheese Turkey Balls 20

G

Galician-Style Octopus 64
Garbanzo Stew with Onions & Tomatoes 103
Garlic & Thyme Pork 39
Garlic Lamb with Thyme 48
Garlic Mushroom Polenta 75
Garlic Red Bell Pepper Sauce 79
German-Style Red Cabbage with Apples 40
Ginger & Garlic Crab 57
Gingery Carrot Soup 84
Grandma's Egg Salad 76
Greek-Style Pasta Salad 78
Green Vegetables with Tomatoes 10
Gruyere Mushroom & Mortadella Cups 40

H

Habanero Chicken Stew 101
Hazelnut Brown Rice Pilaf 67
Herbed Squash Sauce 79
Herby Crab Legs with Lemon 57
Homemade Chicken Puttanesca 12
Homemade Honey Applesauce 81
Homemade Turkey Pepperoni Pizza 23
Homemade Walnut Layer Cake 111
Honey Oat & Pumpkin Granola 72
Honey-Glazed Turkey 35
Hot Beef Chili 102
Hot Paprika & Oregano Lamb 45
Hot Spinach Soup 93
Hot Tofu Meatballs 107
Hungarian-Style Turkey Stew 31

I

Indian Prawn Curry 56
Indian-Style Chicken 15

J

Jamaican Chicken with Pineapple Sauce 11
Jamaican Cornmeal Porridge 74

K

Kielbasa Sausage Soup 87
Kiwi Steel Cut Oatmeal 73

L

Lamb Chops with Mashed Potatoes 52
Lamb Chorba 54
Lamb Shanks with Garlic & Thyme 43
Lamb Stew with Lemon & Parsley 47
Lamb with Tomato & Green Peas 43
Leg of Lamb with Garlic and Pancetta 49
Lemon & Thyme Chicken 19
Lime & Honey Scallops 63

M

Mediterranean Duck with Olives 34
Mediterranean Lamb 46
Mediterranean Tomato Sauce 80
Minty Lamb 44
Moroccan-Style Chicken 17
Mussels With Lemon & White Wine 60
Mustard Carrot Soup 82
Mustard Potato Soup with Crispy Bacon 86

N

North African Turkey Stew 33
Nutmeg Broccoli Soup with Cheddar 87

O

Octopus & Shrimp with Collard Greens 64
One-Pot Mexican Rice 71

P

Pancetta & Cheese Chicken Thighs 101
Parsley & Lemon Turkey Risotto 25
Pecorino Mushroom Soup 96

Peppered Chicken with Chunky Salsa 18
Pilau Brown Rice 69
Plum & Almond Dessert 111
Pomegranate Rice with Vegetables 67
Potato & Cauliflower Turkey Soup 32
Potato Skins with Shredded Turkey 28
Potatoes & Tuna Salad with Pickles 76
Prawn Basmati Rice 66
Pumpkin Steel Cut Oats with Cinnamon 8

Q

Quick Chicken Soup 97
Quick Coconut Treat with Pears 110
Quick French-Style Lamb with Sesame 46
Quick Zucchini Sauce with Greek Yogurt 80

R

Rabbit & Veggie Stew 99
Ranch Potatoes with Ham 41
Red Wine Squid 59
Rice & Chicken Soup 70
Rice & Red Bean Pot 70
Rigatoni with Turkey & Tomato Sauce 22
Roast Goose with White Wine 35
Roast Lamb Leg with Potatoes 42

S

Sage Turkey & Red Wine Casserole 26
Saucy Clams with Herbs 62
Savory Irish Lamb Stew 49
Savory Roast Beef Sandwiches 7
Scallion Chicken & Lentil Soup 85
Simple Apple Cider with Orange Juice 109
Simple Onion Cheese Soup 98
Simple Roast Lamb 47
Southern Cheese Grits 73
Spiced & Warming Mulled Wine 109
Spicy Green Sauce 81
Spicy Ground Beef Soup 92
Spicy Ground Turkey Chili with Vegetables 26
Spicy Indian Rice 69
Spicy Lamb & Bean Chili 51
Spicy Mussels & Anchovies with Rice 61
Spicy Turkey Casserole with Tomatoes 24
Sticky Teriyaki Chicken 14
Sunday Turkey Lettuce Wraps 23
Sweet & Spicy BBQ Chicken 12
Sweet Polenta with Pistachios 104

T

Tamarind Beef Soup 95
Tangy Pumpkin Soup 90
Thyme Chicken Pot with Cheese 100
Tomato Shrimp Soup 85
Traditional Lamb with Vegetables 48
Turkey & Black Bean Chili 27
Turkey Cakes with Ginger Gravy 21
Turkey Meatball Soup with Rice 30
Turkey Sausage with Brussels Sprouts 32
Turkey Soup with Noodle 28
Turkey Stew with Salsa Verde 27
Turkey with Rice & Peas 34
Turkish-Style Roasted Turkey 24

V

Vegan Sloppy Joe's 104
Vegan Tomato Soup 89
Vegetable & Lamb Casserole 53
Vegetable Green Biryani 68

W

Walnut & Dark Chocolate Brownies 110
Weekend Turkey with Vegetables 33
White Wine Marinated Squid Rings 59
White Wine Oysters 65
Wild Rice Pilaf 68

Y

Yummy Vegetable Soup 10

Z

Za'atar Chicken with Baby Potatoes 14

Milton Keynes UK
Ingram Content Group UK Ltd.
UKHW030623160224
437849UK00001B/9